LECTURES

ON THE

NINTH OF ROMANS;

ELECTION,

AND THE

INFLUENCE OF THE HOLY SPIRIT.

By REV ASA MAHAN, A. M.,
PRESIDENT OF THE OBERLIN COLLEGIATE INSTITUTE.

———

1851.

CONTENTS.

	PAGE.
INTRODUCTION BY THE PRESENT EDITOR,	5,
INTRODUCTORY PREFACE,	34,

LECTURE I.
PRELIMINARY OBSERVATIONS, 42,
EXPLANATION OF ROMANS IX.

LECTURE II.
RECAPITULATION, 66,
EXPLANATION OF ROMANS IX.

LECTURE III.
RECAPITULATION, 81,
EXPLANATION OF ROMANS IX.

LECTURE IV.
GENERAL RECAPITULATION, 103,
EXPLANATION OF ROMANS IX.
REMARKS,

LECTURE V.
ELECTION.
PRELIMINARY OBSERVATIONS, 122
PASSAGES IN WHICH THE TERMS "ELECT," "ELECTION," ETC., ARE FOUND EXPLAINED,
OTHER PASSAGES SUPPOSED TO TEACH THIS DOCTRINE EXPLAINED, 134

LECTURE VI.
THE SPIRIT'S INFLUENCES.
DIFFERENT THEORIES STATED,	146
FIRST THEORY,	147
SECOND THEORY,	154
THIRD THEORY,	156
FOURTH THEORY,	157
FIFTH THEORY,	159
SIXTH THEORY,	160
REMARKS,	165

APPENDIX.
LISTING OF WORKS BY ASA MAHAN, 167

INTRODUCTION BY THE PRESENT EDITOR.

DURING one of Mahan's visits to England he was agitated by the universal practice among English clergymen appealing to sinners to be passive about salvation with absurd necessarian notions of inability. As in all of his writings, our author gives us a unique and sound presentation of what he believed to be the need of the hour. Unlike many defenders of the freedom of the will it will be seen that he uses no weak and inconclusive arguments, but reather he gives us a fresh and comprehensive look at the context of Roman's Nine and traces all of the facts in harmony with Paul's clear purpose. Instead of seeking to overthrow a contrary system by the *length* or *amount* of argumentation, he gives us a unique refutation of not only each *essential* argument of the fatalistic or necessarian system, but reveals to us the reasons for their adopting the faulty methods that lead to their belief. He shows us that the main problems in such reasonings have been owning to a wrong *method* used in theology, and in viewing the Bible, that assumes a contradictory system of mental philosophy, and in regards to the Bible, taking verses totally out of context. In this work, as in his many works on Mental Philosophy,[1] he again demonstrates how *any method* ends up with its resulting conclusion as succinctly put by Cousin: "As is the method of a philosopher, so will be his system; and the adoption of a method, decides the destiny of a philosophy." In the same way Mahan shows here: "As is a man's Philosophy so is his Theology." And as is a man's theology so will be his understanding of every verse of the Bible. The circle methodology amounts to *what you put in is what you will get out of it:* fatalism assumed, fatalism resulting. As one of the greatest teachers of mental science of his century, his analysis is worthy of special attention.

---

[1] See the Appendix listing of complete Works by Asa Mahan.

Mahan not only gives us a *theoretical* exposition of this necessarian system of theology and its contradiction to the Ninth of Romans, but gives us the *practical* outworkings of this philosophy in his day, and as it had influenced him in his first thirty years of his life. After some twenty years of painstaking reflection and reexamination—not to mention over fifteen years of teaching Mental Philosophy and Theology—he gives us this critical exposition of one of the most misunderstood chapters of the bible. This is an important consideration in understanding the *motives* behind his writing on this subject. There is no element of bitterness or unkindness in his opposition to this contrary system as has been the case with many *anti-Calvinists;* nor is there any lack of appreciation for the piety of people that held to such systems. As this was all fully developed in his Autobiography, which was written thirty years after this publication, we give you a small segment from that Introduction, along with the first chapter to guide you in understanding the practical outworkings of his former adoption of the belief system he here explains and contrasts to what he considers to be the true system of Theology: [2]

'During my religious life, I have had a very intimate association with the various religious, moral, social, and political questions and movements which have agitated and moulded thought in America and the world at large, and with many of the leading minds who gave form and direction to these great movements. As a student of theology and Biblical science, and of all the sciences, as a preacher of the everlasting Gospel, and as a Professor of Mental and Moral Philosophy and Theology, I have had occasion to ponder, and weigh, and determine, with great care and circumspection, the various problems of natural, mental, moral, and theological science, together with the doctrines of the diverse schools in philosophy and religion. As a theologian I have, as the result of the most careful and candid inquiry and research, passed from the extreme bounds of Calvinism to the quite opposite pole of the evangelical faith.'

---

[2] *Autobiography; Intellectual, Moral, and Spiritual.* Republication by Alethea In Heart, 2001, p. 9, from the Introduction; Chapter I, pp. 12-36.

PHILOSOPHY AND RELIGION IN AMERICA
AN ALETHEA IN HEART PUBLICATION
IN THE SERIES OF
THE LIFE AND WORKS OF ASA MAHAN.

1. Doctrine of the Will. 1847.
2. The System of Mental Philosophy. 1882.
3. A System of Intellectual Philosophy. 1854.
4. The Science of Logic; or an Analysis of the Laws of Thought. 1857.
5. Science of Moral Philosophy. 1848.
6. 7. A Critical History of Philosophy in two Volumes. 1883.
8. The Science of Natural Theology. 1867.
9. Autobiography: Intellectual, Moral, and Spiritual. 1882.
10. The True Believer. 1847.
11. Scripture Doctrine of Christian Perfection. 1837, 1875.
12. Out of Darkness Into Light. 1877.
13. Baptism of the Holy Ghost. 1875.
14. Misunderstood Texts of Scripture. 1876.
15. Life Thoughts on the Rest of Faith. 1872.
16. Lectures on the Ninth of Romans. 1859.
17. The Phenomena of Spiritism; and, Spiritualism a Discussion. 1875.
18. Modern Mysteries Examined and Exposed. 1855.
19. A Critical History of the Late American War. 1877.
20. Miscellaneous Articles, Letters, and Index of the Complete Works.

LECTURES ON THE NINTH OF ROMANS

REPUBLISHED BY THE EDITOR.
RICHARD FRIEDRICH OF
ALETHEA IN HEART MINISTRIES
PO BOX 127 Charlotte, MI 48813
TruthInHeart.com
(208) 304-2954

March 2002.

Mahan, Asa, 1800-1889.
Lectures on the Ninth of Romans; Election, and the Influence of the Holy Spirit.

Republication of the 1851 ed. Published by Charles H. Peirce & Company, Boston.
1. English and Calvinistic Preaching. 2. Exposition of Romans IX. 3. The Necessarian Philosophy. 4. Ancient and Modern forms of Judaism. 5. Election. 6. Predestination Conditional. 7. Biblical Election. 8. Six Theories of Divine Influence in Conversion. 9. Inability in Conversion. 10. Limited Atonement.

ISBN 1-932370-13-7

First Alethea In Heart edition published in 2002.
Second Alethea In Heart edition published in 2016.
Reproduced from the edition of 1851,
Boston, without altering anything but format and page numbers.

Copyright © 2002, 2016
Richard Max Friedrich
All Rights Reserved

MANUFACTURED IN THE UNITED STATES OF AMERICA

'EARLY RELIGIOUS IMPRESSIONS.

'IT was at the age of seventeen years and two or three months that I was born of God. The reader will better understand and appreciate the intellectual, moral, and spiritual life to which he is about to be introduced, if we go back to the period which immediately preceded the event above referred to, and consider the specific religious convictions and impressions to which I was then subject, together with the character of the causes of those convictions and impressions.

'Early Education.

'My education from my childhood up was, especially in a *doctrinal* sense, a religious one. The circle in which I was educated was exclusively Calvinistic of the" straitest sect" ever known. Always a regular attendant upon public worship on the Sabbath, I had never, up to the period of my life now under consideration, heard more than two or three discourses from any preacher who did not belong to this school. As soon as I was able to read at all, the first treatises put into my hands were the Assembly's Longer and Shorter Catechisms. The latter I was required to commit to memory, and to repeat to my mother from Sabbath to Sabbath, that is, very frequently, during the years of childhood. From the teachings of these catechisms and other forms of religious instruction, my views of Christian doctrine very early took a definite and systematic character. Being naturally endued with a reflective mind, and especially with a quenchless thirst for knowledge, and especially for the knowledge possessed by intelligent men and women around me, I was ever a most attentive and eager listener to their varied conversations, conversations especially which pertained to two subjects,—battles, and questions of Christian doctrine; and no child was more favoured than I was in gaining the best information of the latter kind. My mother was one of the greatest female thinkers and readers on religious topics that I ever knew. No minister in all the region of country where we lived was more fully acquainted with the writings of such thinkers as Edwards, Hopkins, Bellamy, and Emmons, than she. My father's house was consequently the centre for the discussion of Christian doctrine with the most intelligent members of the church to which he and my mother belonged. Western New York, where my parents lived from my twelfth to my seventeenth year, was, at that time, for the most part, missionary ground. Scattered in all directions were feeble churches without pastoral care. These churches were favoured from time to time with the temporary services of missionaries sent out for the most part from the State of Connecticut. Standing on one of the main roads and near the centre of the town, my father's house was the fixed stopping place of these missionaries. How my heart would leap when a stranger would ride up to my father's door, and announce himself a missionary from the State of Connecticut. "Now," I inwardly exclaimed, "we shall have more conversation about these doctrines;" and I was never disappointed. As soon as the proper time for conversation came, my mother, who was a woman of few words herself, would put some leading questions which would arouse to the highest degree the mental activity of the visitor, and insure a most animated discussion of some of the great doctrines. Not unfrequently more or less of the neighbours would come in and heighten the interest of the discussions. Sometimes two such strangers would call at the same time, and then the interest of the collisions of thought would reach its climax. To all such scenes there was sure to be one listener whose attention and interest never flagged. The church of which my parents were members, never, during the period under consideration, enjoyed public preaching except on alternate Sabbaths; on all other Sabbaths they had what were called "Reading Meetings," meetings in which two printed discourses were read aloud. The discourses selected represented what was then universally regarded as embodying the best thoughts of the best Calvinistic divines of the age, and in each discourse some phase of some one of the great doctrines was elucidated. Whenever any new volume was introduced, my mother was certain to borrow it and read its discourses through, and always aloud when I was present. I therefore usually heard all such discourses twice read, and listened with the strictest attention.

'Even after I was eight or ten years of age I was much given to religious thought and reflection. I seriously question whether, after this period, I was for half an hour alone by myself without pondering more or less seriously some forms of religious thought. I refer to the above facts in order to evince that I must have been an inexpressibly stupid thinker had I not, under such influences, attained to very clear, distinct, and definite apprehensions of all the leading doctrines of the system of faith in which I was educated. That my apprehensions were not only clear and definite, but strictly correct, I argue from the two following considerations: 1. No one ever suggested to me the thought—not even my mother, who ever had an open view of all my religious thinking—no one ever hinted to me, that I had misapprehended at all any of those doctrines. 2. My subsequent theological reading and education never suggested to me the idea that I had, in any particular, misapprehended the nature of any of those doctrines. I have fundamentally changed my views of the accordance of those doctrines with the Word of God, but never in respect to what is their intrinsic nature and character.

'Religious Convictions and Impressions induced by these Doctrines.

'What now were the religious convictions and impressions induced in my mind by a most careful and impartial view of these doctrines? I use the term *impartial* because I never entertained the prejudices entertained against them by worldly minds around me. I accepted them as truths of God, which I could not change, and by objecting against which I could only injure myself. I recollect very well an argument presented in one of the discourses which I heard read; an argument which, for years, utterly silenced in my mind all objection against the doctrine that infinite criminality is set down to the account of every individual of the race on account of the one sin of Adam. The argument was this: Had Adam maintained his integrity, and had God, on account of the merits of his obedience, set down to the account of each individual of the race the desert of infinite good, no creature in earth or heaven would have objected. Why, then, should any one object to the fact, that on account of Adam's sin infinite demerit is set down to the account of every such individual? Years passed before an objection arose in my mind to this doctrine of imputation. Thus candidly and impartially did I contemplate all the doctrines under consideration. I speak, also, of the impressions arising from a consideration of these doctrines. I had other religious convictions and impressions induced in my mind by other facts and considerations; and to these I shall direct special attention hereafter. What we are now to consider is *the convictions and impressions induced by an exclusive consideration of these doctrines themselves.*

'What, then, were these convictions and impressions? *An utter and absolute exclusion,* I answer, *of all ideas of real duty, obligation, merit or demerit of good or ill, from the entire sphere of Christian truth, thought, and action.* This, I affirm unqualifiedly, was the exact state induced in my mind by those years of careful study of those doctrines. That I was under condemnation to eternal death, on account of the one sin of Adam, which God had imputed to me, I entertained not the remotest doubt. Yet that I was, in any sense or form, morally responsible for that sin, that real *desert* of punishment did, or could, attach to me personally on account of it, or that I was in the remotest degree under obligation to repent of the same,—no such thought or sentiment ever approached my mind. The sin and its imputed penalty lay, in my thoughts and reflections, wholly outside the circle of personal responsibility or desert; as much so as did the Flood, and the crimes of the generations which preceded and occasioned that world catastrophe.

'Equally absolute was my, conviction that through the fall of Adam, and by a Divinely established law of natural descent, my "whole nature was corrupted" and "disabled to all that is good;" that what is "commonly called original sin" was to me and all the race a dire reality, a reality on account of which an eternal doom hung over myself and all the race. Yet I intuitively imputed original sin to myself and to the race as a pure calamity, and never, in any sense, as a crime. I was familiar with the fact of hereditary diseases descending through parents to their children, through successive generations. The child in whom such disease appears, is always compassionated, and never regarded as really criminal, for being afflicted with such disease; and that even when it is known that the parent brought upon himself the disease by crime. So I intuitively regarded, "the corruption of our whole nature, which is commonly called original sin."

'That I was a sinner, originally and actually so, I had no doubt, and fully believed my catechism, when it affirmed that "all sin, both original and actual, being a transgression of the Divine law, deserves God's wrath and curse, both in this world and that which is to come." The term *deserves* had no meaning in my regard but this, *is doomed to receive.* The term *sin,* as employed in theological and Christian discourse, represented nothing whatever for which I regarded myself as, in the remotest degree, responsible. When spoken to of particular outward actions as right or wrong, or as deserving of praise or blame, my conscience gave a ready response to the correctness of such imputations. But when *sin* was spoken of, sin which, I was then taught, consisted in inward natural corruption, or in positive states or acts necessarily resulting from "indwelling sin," all conviction of real responsibility for such corruption, states, or acts, wholly dropped out of my mind, or rather never became a matter of conviction at all.

'The same held true of all the specific requirements of religion, such as repentance, faith, love, and religious service. I was well aware that these were immutable conditions of salvation; that without "repentance toward God, and faith toward our Lord Jesus Christ," I should be eternally lost. Yet the conviction that I *ought* to repent and believe never had place in my mind. I was fully aware that "I must be born again, or I could not see the kingdom of God." I had no more consciousness of any obligation to become a Christian, however, than I had to become an angel.

'I saw nothing whatever in the character of God, as seen through these doctrines, let me add once more, nothing whatever which awakened in my mind for a moment the conviction, in any sense or form, that I *ought* to love Him. I knew that I was required to love Him, and must do it, or be lost eternally. As presented to my apprehensions, there was everything in God to inspire awe, fear, and dread, but nothing to attract and to love. All His thoughts, plans, purposes, works, and government had their beginning, middle, and end wholly within Himself. He loved His creatures, and valued their interests, as the potter delights in and values his clay, as something to which he can give mould and shape to meet his own personal ends. So, as I was taught, God, by His omnipotence, gives existence to creatures, determines their character, lives, and destiny, forms and moulds them as vessels of honour or dishonour in absolute subordination to one exclusive end, His own pleasure, or "glory," as it was called. With what awe, and dread, and freezing terror, and with no love drawings, did we hear such stanzas sung as the following!

> "Keep silence, all created things,
> And wait your Maker's nod.
> My soul stands trembling while she sings
> The honours of her God.

> "Chain'd to His throne a volume lies,
> With all the fates of men,
> With every angel's form and size,
> Drawn by the eternal pen.

> "Not Gabriel asks the reason why,

> Nor God the reason gives
> Nor dares the favoured angel pry
> Between the folded leaves."

'Thus it was that, through the religious teachings which I received, and the doctrines which were continuously held before my mind, and so deeply pondered by me, all real sentiments of religious obligation, all real convictions of duty, and all real consciousness of moral desert, were utterly excluded from the sphere of Christian thought and reflection, in which my mind had its dwelling-place. Had I been possessed of no conscience or moral nature at all, there could not have been a more absolute exclusion from my mind and thoughts of all such sentiments and convictions.

These Convictions and Impressions the necessary logical Consequents of the Doctrines in which I had been instructed.

'We will now advance to a consideration of these doctrines themselves, and inquire whether the convictions and impressions under consideration were or were not the necessary logical consequents of what is intrinsic in the doctrines through which these convictions and impressions were intuitively induced in my mind. To set the subject distinctly before the reader, permit me to invite special attention to the following fact. Some twenty-five or thirty years since, when in the city of New York, I learned that a relative of mine, the wife of a wealthy merchant in that city, was in a precarious state of health. I had known her from childhood, and for many reasons she was very dear to me. She, as was true of myself, had from childhood been educated under the exclusive influence of these doctrines. Regarding this as probably my last opportunity for conversation with my niece, 1 called for one exclusive purpose,—a serious conversation with her on the interests of her soul's eternity. When this subject was introduced, she frankly confessed to me that she was not a Christian. "The question of my salvation," she added, "in no sense or form lies with myself but wholly at the sovereign disposal of God. If I am not one of the elect, my doom is fixed and irreversible, and I can do nothing to change it. If I am one of the elect, the time of my conversion is immutably determined, and I can do nothing to hasten or put it off. When that time shall arrive, God will send His Spirit to renew my heart, and it will be absolutely impossible for me to resist Him, or prevent my conversion. I have nothing to do, and can do nothing in the matter." "My dear, precious niece," I exclaimed, "reasoning thus and acting thus you will lose your soul, as sure as you exist." This only convinced her that I was a teacher of error. I found her mind, as my own had been, a total blank, as far as any proper convictions of sin, or any religious sentiments of duty and moral desert, were concerned, and all through the exclusive influence of the doctrines in which she had been educated. Whether any change occurred in her experience prior to her death, which took place but a few months after my visit, I never learned. Was this utter extinguishment of such convictions and impressions the necessary logical consequence of the doctrines under consideration? This is the question before us.

'In the forefront of all these doctrines stands that of the Divine Decrees, which is thus defined in the Assembly's Catechism "The decrees of God are His eternal purpose, according to the counsel of His own will, whereby, for His own glory, He foreordained whatsoever comes to pass." "God executes His decrees," it is added, "in the works of creation and providence." "God's works of providence," we further read, "are His most holy, wise, and powerful preserving and governing all His creatures, and all their actions." "The almighty power, unsearchable wisdom, and infinite goodness of God, so far manifest themselves in His providence," says the Confession of Faith, "that it (His providence) extendeth itself even to the first fall, and all actions of angels and of men and that not by a mere permission, but such as hath joined with it a most wise and powerful bounding and otherwise ordering and governing of them in a manifold dispensation to His own holy ends." Here we are taught that all events, including all the actions of all beings, were, from eternity, immutably predetermined by God Himself; and that in providence He employs His omnipotence to bring those absolutely predetermined events to pass. No events, then, thus predetermined can, by any possibility, fail to occur, and to occur just as predetermined, and no events not predetermined can by any possibility occur. The absolute and exclusive Determiner is God: the determined are all existences and events, the nature, mental states, and actions of all creatures included. Granting the facts as here stated—and they must be thus granted, if this doctrine is true—where, in the necessary judgment of the universal conscience and intelligence, must all moral responsibility, moral obligation, and moral desert, if they exist anywhere, be exclusively located?

Must they be located with the absolute and exclusive Determiner, or with the absolutely determined? Holding that doctrine as true, my conscience and reason and intelligence intuitively denied of myself all personal obligation and moral desert. So, these being the only premises from which to judge, must the conscience and reason and intelligence of every rational being decide. We can no more conceive that obligation and moral desert lie exclusively with the absolutely determined, and not with the absolute and exclusive Determiner, than we can conceive of an event without a cause.

'Next in order after the Divine decrees, we will consider the condition of the human race in consequence of the fall of Adam, as set forth in the system under consideration. The fall, we must bear in mind, was according to this system as absolutely fixed and predetermined by a Divine decree as any other event. Adam, by an irresistible overruling providence, was placed in a state of probation, in which, as a foreordained event, his fall could not but occur. What is the affirmed state of the race consequent on that fall? "The covenant," says the Catechism, "being made with Adam, not only for himself but for his posterity, all mankind, descending from him by ordinary generation, sinned in him, and fell with him in his first transgression." "The fall," we are further told, "brought mankind into a state of sin and misery." Again "The sinfulness of that estate whereinto man fell, consists in the guilt of Adam's first sin, the want of original righteousness, and the corruption of his whole nature, which is commonly called original sin, together with all actual transgressions, which proceed from it." Once more: "All mankind by the fall lost communion with God, are under His wrath and curse, and so made liable to all the miseries of this life, to death itself, and to the pains of hell for ever." In another connection, we were taught, that "all sin, both original and actual, being contrary to the law of God, deserves His wrath and curse, both in this world and that which is to come." Again: "The sinfulness of that estate wherein man fell consisteth in the guilt of Adam's first sin, the want of that righteousness wherein he was created, and the corruption of his nature, whereby he is utterly indisposed, disabled, made opposite to all that is spiritually good, and wholly inclined to all that is evil, and that continually." "Man by his fall hath lost all ability of will to any spiritual good."

'For each of three distinct and separate reasons, infinite criminality is, according to the doctrine under consideration, set down to the account of each individual of the race, namely: I. For a single act of one individual, an act perpetrated thousands of years before a vast majority of them existed at all. 2. For the original possession of a fallen nature, in the origination of which they had no more agency direct or indirect than they had in the creation of the world; a fallen nature which God Himself originated through the laws of natural generation. 3. For actual transgressions which the fallen nature of which mankind thus became possessed, rendered it absolutely impossible for them not to commit. For these specific reasons I did regard myself as thus doomed. My reason and conscience, however, absolutely cleared me of all real criminality in the matter, so absolutely that the thought that I could be really criminal for the sin of Adam which was imputed to me, or for sin in any form, original or actual, never entered my mind. Why did my conscience and intellectual and moral nature thus intuitively judge? For the absolute reason, I answer, that that judgment is the necessary logical deduction from the doctrines themselves.

'The pastor of a leading church in an American city, a church of which my own daughter was a member, after stating these doctrines just as I have done, added that while he fully believed in these doctrines, in the ill-desert of sin, and in the duty of repentance, it was absolutely impossible for him to conceive *how* the creature can be responsible for sin, or under obligation to repent of it. He could conceive of no such possibility, I answer, for the simple and exclusive reason, that the thing is an absolute impossibility. The intuition is not more absolute that a circle is not a square, than is the judgment that if those doctrines are true, obligation and moral desert are impossibilities.

'State of Infants who die before they are capable of committing actual Sin.

'Infants who die before they can possibly commit actual sin, die, according to the express teaching of the system under consideration, under the desert of "God's wrath and curse" to eternity, for two fundamental reasons; namely, the guilt of Adam's sin which is imputed to them; and "original sin," or "the want of original righteousness, and the corruption of their whole nature." According to my absolute intuitive apprehensions, while I regarded such desert as actually imputed to all such persons, there was, and could be, no *real* desert of such punishment, or of any punishment at all, in such cases. We have, in fact and form, the absolute verdict of human reason and conscience inside and outside the Church in respect to this particular case. And what is this verdict? The doctrine was once openly maintained, that infants dying in such state were of two classes, elect and non-elect; and that the latter, for the two specific reasons above designated, were actually doomed to eternal misery. The doctrine was so shocking to the reason and conscience and moral nature of universal mind, sanctified and unsanctified, that this doctrine of infant damnation has been frowned with indignation and reprobation out of the Church, and it is now confessed with shame that any such horror ever had place in Christian belief. What is the reason that this doctrine is universally held in such utter reprobation? The reason, and the only reason, is that according to the absolute intuition of the universal reason and conscience, no such desert, no desert of punishment of any kind, does or can attach to a moral being for the reasons assigned. If such desert for such reasons does exist, and is perceived to exist, there should be nothing morally shocking to any mind in the idea that such punishment is actually inflicted. The idea that any being receives what and no more than he actually deserves, shocks the reason and conscience of no moral agent. Either the intelligence and conscience and moral nature as God has constituted them are a lie, or no desert of eternal doom, or real desert of punishment in any form, does or can attach to infants, or to men now living, for that first sin of Adam or for any mere inherited constitutional temperaments.

Doctrine of Election, Reprobation, Regeneration, &c.

'We will now consider the doctrines of election, reprobation, regeneration, and kindred doctrines, as set forth in the system under discussion. "By the decree of God," says the Confession of Faith, "for the manifestation of His glory, some men and angels are predestinated unto everlasting life, and others foreordained to everlasting death." "These angels and men, thus predestinated and foreordained, are particularly and unchangeably designed; and their number is so certain and definite that it cannot be either increased or diminished." "Effectual call is of God's free and special grace alone, not for anything at all foreseen in man; who is altogether passive therein, until, being quickened and renewed by the Holy Spirit, he is thereby enabled to answer the call, and to embrace the grace offered and conveyed therein." "Elect infants, dying in infancy, are regenerated and saved by Christ through the Spirit,

Who worketh where and when and how He pleaseth." "All the elect, and they only, are effectually called."

'As regeneration and effectual calling were affirmed to be the exclusive work of the Spirit, a change in which the creature is "wholly passive," I was accustomed to hear aged, intelligent, and experienced believers affirm that the Spirit could regenerate an individual when asleep as well as at any other time. And where can an error be found in such utterances, if the doctrine on which they are based is true?

'Now, taking into account the doctrines of the Divine decrees, of the fall, of election, regeneration, and effectual calling, as actually set forth in the system under consideration, who will deny that the necessary logical consequent is the absolute validity of the conviction that rested upon my mind, that I was in reality under no more real obligation to become a Christian than I was to become an angel; that no more real *desert* of punishment did or could attach to me for the fall of Adam than for the fall of Satan; and that in no sense or form was I responsible, that is, deserving of punishment, for sin, whether original or actual? Can any one feel surprise that I deliberately regarded all charges of guilt on account of sin, and all affirmed obligations to repent of it and enter upon a holy life, as absurd mockeries? I distinctly recollect saying within myself, when our deacon charged such things upon us, "Now, Deacon B. is mocking us. He knows that what he is saying is not true."

'The reader can now understand clearly the validity of my conviction, that the character of God, as presented in this system, wears one exclusive aspect,—infinite selfism, valuing His creatures but as the potter values his clay, as objects which, by His own power, He can form and dispose of for His own ends. For what exclusive end did God, as we are here taught, foreordain whatsoever comes to pass? For His own glory. Why did He elect a portion of our fallen race to eternal life? For His own glory. Why did He from eternity determine to pass by the non-elect, and leave them to perish in their sins? For His own glory. If we should become "followers of God" in conformity to such a revelation of His character, our selfism would be as absolute as His.

'Different and opposite Schools of Calvinism.

'At the period to which I now refer, Calvinists were divided into three schools; the division in the Presbyterian Church into Old School and New School not having then occurred. Of the three schools then existing the first held, in the strictest form, the doctrines above considered, as set forth in the catechisms, and its creed was commonly represented by the terms "limited atonement" and "inability; "the latter term having reference to its tenet that all men are, by original sin, *disabled* from all good acts.

The doctrine of the second school was denominated "Hopkinsianism; "the Rev. Samuel Hopkins, D.D., of Newport, Rd., in connection with President Edwards, being its principal expounder and advocate. This school agreed in all essential respects with the first-named, as far as the doctrine of the fall is concerned. In opposition to a *limited,* Hopkinsianism maintained a *general* atonement, affirming that provisions of grace in Christ are for the entire race, and are as free for the acceptance of the non-elect as for the elect. In opposition to the doctrine of absolute inability, this school affirmed that all men, the non-elect as well as the elect, have *natural* but not *moral* ability to accept the offer of life and obey the will of God. It was a common saying among believers of this school that, although their eternal doom is fixed by an eternal decree of God, the non-elect have natural power, by accepting the provisions of grace, to insure their salvation by breaking the Divine decrees. According to the teaching of this school, also, the *common* influences of the Spirit, those under which none are ever converted, are given to all men without exception. His *special* influences, on the other hand, those which always when vouchsafed result in conversion, God, in the exercise of His sovereignty, withholds from the non-elect and confers upon the elect. While the common influences of the Spirit never result in conversion, they do infinitely aggravate the criminality and doom of the non-elect. All men, the non-elect included, have natural ability to obey God, because nothing hinders their doing so, and assuring their own salvation, but their unwillingness. They lack moral power, because they have no power over their own choices; that is, they choose the evil and refuse the good, without the power of contrary choice. The distinction between this doctrine of natural ability and moral inability, and that of absolute inability as maintained by hyper-Calvinists, as they were then called, was found, when the two doctrines were clearly understood, to be in reality a distinction without a difference; the common doctrine of each school being that unregenerate men have no *available* power whatever to obey God. No school maintained the doctrine of eternal decrees and of unconditional election in a more absolute form than did that under consideration. In all His works and government God has, we were taught, but one exclusive end,—His own glory, the display of His perfections. To this end it is as necessary that some should eternally sin and suffer, as that others should be eternally holy and happy; and God from eternity elected His vessels of mercy and vessels of wrath according to His sovereign pleasure. By the founder and leading advocates of this school, it was most strongly maintained that such should be our regard for the sovereign will of our Maker, that "we should be willing to be damned for the glory of God." A bound volume of an old magazine in my library at home contains an article written by myself in defence of this doctrine. The doctrine of general atonement and natural ability, as maintained by this school, was hailed by multitudes of ministers and believers as a fundamental advance in the direction of rational Christian truth, and as rolling an incubus of infinite weight from Christian doctrine.

'The doctrine of the third school, which was founded by the Rev. Nathaniel Emmons, D.D., was denominated "the Divine Efficiency Scheme." In all points in which the second school differed from the first, this last agreed with the former, and rejected the doctrines of the latter. In contradistinction from the teachings of each of the first two schools, this last denied and denounced the doctrines of the imputation of Adam's sin, and of all desert of punishment for "original sin," maintaining that men are and can be justly held responsible but for their own voluntary acts of obedience or disobedience to the revealed will of God. The peculiarity of the system was, that it maintained that in conformity with an eternal decree God, by the direct exertion of His own omnipotence, originates all human volitions and acts, the holy and the sinful in common. Thus God, by the direct and immediate exertion of His own omnipotence, moulds the character and determines the destiny of the elect and non-elect. Thus also, according to the bald teaching of this school, teaching which had among its open advocates not a few of the ablest thinkers in the United States, God holds all sinners as deserving, and actually inflicts upon the non-elect eternal doom, for acts which He, by the direct exertion of His own omnipotence, renders it absolutely impossible for them not to put forth.

'Such were the doctrines of these three schools, which included all Calvinists at that time. The doctrine common to them all was that of Necessity, that all human activity cannot but be, in all respects, what it is. Now, while the doctrines of each of these schools were condemned by the united verdict of the universal intelligence outside of the schools themselves, as utterly subversive of all righteous legislation, human and Divine, of all obligation and moral desert of every kind, making God the only responsible Being, each of them denounced, in exactly the same forms, the doctrines of each of the others. "The idea that God," exclaimed the hyper-Calvinist and Hopkinsian, "by the direct action of His own omnipotence, originates all human volitions and acts, imputes infinite criminality to the Almighty, and renders Him the most fell tyrant conceivable." Just such language I often heard at that time, and no direct reply was ever made to the imputation. The following was the mode in which the advocate of Divine efficiency replied to the objections of the opposite schools. "You affirm that the doctrine that God imputes infinite criminality to sinners for acts of transgression which He, by the direct action of His own omnipotence, renders it impossible for them not to commit, dishonours Him. What then must we think of your doctrine, that God imputes to all men the desert of eternal doom for a sin which they never committed at all, and also for the possession of a depraved nature, in the origination of which they had no agency whatever, direct or indirect, but which God Himself, by the direct exertion of His own omnipotence, did originate through the laws of natural generation? If it would imply infinite wrong in God to impute infinite guilt to men for acts which He directly originates in them, and necessitates them to commit, would it not imply equal wrong for Him to hold them thus guilty for actual sins, which the fallen nature which He thus imparted to them renders it impossible for them not to commit?"

'On a visit to Dr. Emmons, the Rev. Lyman Beecher, D.D., thus addressed his venerable friend: "You hold and teach, do you not, Dr. Emmons, that God, by the direct exertion of His own omnipotence, actually originates all sinful volitions and acts?" "I do thus hold and teach," was the reply. "Well, Dr. Emmons, there is, to my apprehension, something inexplicably mysterious about this matter, and I would earnestly request you to remove the difficulty. When God, by the direct exertion of almighty power, has originated an act of sin, He seems to be very indignant at what He has Himself created. He also manifests infinite surprise that the event should have occurred at all, and calls upon heaven and earth to unite with Him in astonishment and indignation that an act of obedience does not appear, instead of the sinful one, when He, by the direct exertion of His own omnipotence, renders the appearance of the former, and the non-appearance of the latter, an absolute impossibility. How do you explain such difficulties, Dr. Emmons?" The countenance of the great expounder of the doctrine of Divine efficiency instantly became a total blank. Putting his hand to his forehead, he remained for some time in deep thought, then dropped his hand, and looking in every direction with a bewildered stare, he remained silent. Dr. Beecher was too much of a Christian gentleman to embarrass his venerable friend with further questions, and the subject was dropped. When Dr. Emmons apprehended his own doctrine as it is in itself, the intuition became absolute in his own mind, that the absurdity of that doctrine was infinite. Now the doctrine of each of the schools under consideration does undeniably involve an absurdity as blank and palpable as this, and can by no possibility be so expounded as to be freed from such absurdity.

'I have spoken of the utter exclusion from my mind, through the influence of these doctrines, of all proper conviction of sin as that which actually *deserves* "God's wrath and curse," and of all other kindred convictions. Now this was practically true, not only of worldly minds around me, but of believers also. Even the most devout Christians I knew, when they mentioned their sins, always spoke of them as evincing, not infinite criminality and ill-desert, but feebleness and dependence. They would make confession that all their "righteousnesses were as filthy rags," and that there was no soundness in them; that from their heads to the soles of their feet they were "full of wounds and bruises and putrefying sores," and then, with a placid smile, they would exclaim, "What poor dependent creatures we are!" They always *compassionated,* instead of really *criminating* themselves, when they spoke of their sins. Under a distinct apprehension of these systems, conviction of sin, in its only true and proper form, is an utter impossibility. Many who hold these systems have real conviction of sin, and that because their intuitions, enlightened by the Spirit of God, supersede the influence of doctrinal beliefs.

'Illustrative Incident.

'About forty-seven years since, when I was pastor of a Presbyterian Church in Cincinnati, Ohio, I was invited to attend a Protracted Meeting in the village of Oxford, the seat of a State

University of that name. The pastor of the church where I preached, who was also my host, requested that I would have special religious conversation with a sister-in-law of his, then residing in his family. She was, as he stated, the principal of the ladies' academy in the place, of superior education, of a high order of talents, and most irreproachable morals, but utterly unapproachable on the subject of religion. "The principal motive which I had in securing your present services," he added, "was the hope that you might be instrumental in leading her out of that ice-bound, unapproachable state in which she has been for years." During my first religious conversation with that lady, she made this remark to me: "I see nothing whatever in the character of God, for which my conscience affirms to me that I *ought* to love Him." On my inquiring the origin and cause of such impressions, she stated that years previous, when a pupil at a female academy in New England, she boarded in the family of one of the most influential members of the church in the place. During a revival of religion in the academy she was the subject of very deep religious impressions. In conversation with the gentleman referred to, she was told that if she was not one of the elect, as she very probably was not, her present religious impressions could have but one result,—to render her more a vessel of wrath than she otherwise could become, and that the Spirit was very probably given her for this purpose. Subsequently to this she overheard this man inform some Christian friends that he had made these statements to her, and that he believed they were true. Accepting this as the correct view of her case, her heart at once seemed to be turned into a stone within her, and she had never since felt any disposition whatever to give thought to religious subjects. My prompt and earnest reply, as soon as she had finished her statements, was, "Miss you ought to be sent to perdition. God has given His Son and sent His Spirit to you for one expressly revealed and exclusive purpose, 'that you might not perish, but have everlasting life,' and has affirmed, under oath, that He has 'no pleasure in' your 'death;' that He entertains but one desire in respect to you, and that is your salvation. Yet, in the face of all this, and on the bold assertion of that most presumptuous man, you have for all these years entertained the horrid slander upon your Heavenly Father, that He was dealing with you, not to secure your salvation, but to insure your eternal doom, and render that doom as aggravated as possible. What excuse will you, can you, offer to your injured Father and God, should you appear before

Him in this state, for having made yourself a vessel of wrath by entertaining such soul-ruining thoughts in regard to Him? Go to Him at once, and tell Him frankly and broken-heartedly how you have injured Him, and wronged your own soul, by such thoughts." Perceiving that the ice around the heart was broken, I left her for a short time to her own reflections. At our next interview, after presenting a full statement of "the truth, as it is in Jesus," I put the question directly to her, "Will you now admit that God loves you, desires to confer eternal life upon you, and will do it as soon as you turn to Him, and commend yourself to His grace and mercy?" "I will," was the prompt and earnest reply. On the evening following I preached from the text, "If any man sin, we have an Advocate with the Father, Jesus Christ the Righteous," and showed on what conditions Christ will act in our behalf in this relation, and what He will procure for us if we commit our case to Him. On our way from the meeting I said to our friend, "Miss —, shall Christ he *your* Advocate?" "If I do not accept of Him," was her prompt and earnest reply, "I ought to go to hell. I can plead guilty now. I have but one desire, and that is that Christ may possess and control my whole being." When I left the place she was one of the happiest converts I had ever seen. More than thirty years after that, I met that minister and inquired of him in respect to that sister-in-law. "She died a few months since," was the reply, "but such a life as she led, after your visit to Oxford, I do not know that I ever witnessed. We never saw in her the remotest indication of backsliding, and her Christian character was throughout wonderfully complete and symmetrical. She never shrank from duty in any form, and never appeared to think that she could do enough for Christ. So her life brightened on to the close. And it did seem as if 'heaven had come down to greet,' as we stood about her dying bed."

'Here we have God's truth, as often perverted and misrepresented in the schools, on the one hand, and as revealed in His Divine Word, on the other. Here, too, we have the distinct and opposite results. What that man said to that inquirer was a veritable exposition of the doctrine which he held, and the effect upon her mind was the legitimate outcome of that doctrine. When I had been for several weeks in great anguish of mind on account of my religious condition and prospects, our deacon, who was *de facto* the pastor of our church, fully aware of my state of mind, thus addressed us: "My impenitent friends, bear this in mind, that if any of you were not from eternity elected unto eternal life, your salvation is impossible." When I afterwards spoke to another leading professor upon the subject, his reply was, "I ought to say to you that the statements of Deacon B—— were undoubtedly correct." That my soul was not wrecked for eternity was owing wholly to the mercy and grace of God in counteracting the natural effects of fundamental error. The reason why such teachings were presented to persons "under concern of mind," was the belief then commonly entertained, that in revivals, of all other times, "the doctrines should be fully preached." In after years such teachings were withheld until the revivals had passed by.

'Origin and Character of Early Religious Impressions which led to my Conversion.

'My early religious convictions and impressions were, for very many years after my conversion, a mystery to me; and it was only after long and very mature reflection that I came to fully comprehend their nature and causes. At first thought it would seem likely that systems of doctrine, the belief of which utterly extinguishes and excludes from the mind all proper convictions of real obligation to obey the law of duty and the will of God, of the real ill-desert of sin, and of responsibility to comply with the revealed conditions of eternal life, would as utterly exclude all religious impressions of every kind. In my own case, for example, there was this utter exclusion of proper religious *conviction,* on the one hand, and the very frequent presence of very deep religious *impressions* of another kind, on the other. The real cause of the absence of religious convictions of the kind under consideration has already been explained. The origin, and causes, and character of the *impressions* referred to admit of an equally ready explanation.

'Let us suppose that the entire race has inherited from our first parents a disease, which can by no possibility be removed or modified by human remedies, and which, left to its own course, would, within a limited period, result in death. We have, at the same time, a revelation from God that He has from eternity determined and made provisions to remove this disease from a certain fixed number of the race, His elect, the number of whom cannot be increased or diminished, and at a certain predetermined period to carry them through a certain crisis, from which they will by Divine power pass into a state of permanent health and happiness. The other portion of the race, " persons not elected," God has immutably determined to pass by, and leave under the power of this disease, through which, at the crisis when the elect surmount it and live, if not before, the non-elect die and return to dust. Under such circumstances, while none could or ought to feel any responsibility for their state or destiny, the question, "Do I belong to the number of the elect, or non-elect, the number who are to survive and live, or to die and return to dust?" might be to each a subject of the deepest concern; and when the determining crisis should come, all might, each in his turn, experience not only great physical but mental agony.

'Now, when my mind awoke to a consciousness of myself and the realities around me, I found myself, according to what was taught me, actually under sentence to eternal doom for the act of an ancestor—an act committed near six thousand years before my being commenced—and for a fallen nature derived from that ancestor, a nature in the origin and character of which I had had no more agency than I had had in that first sin. I found myself, also, in consequence of this inherited nature, utterly disabled to all that is good, and with no power to avoid actual transgressions for which infinite retributions were to be inflicted upon me, unless I should be rescued by an Almighty Power above and beyond myself. Here I was met by an affirmed revelation that I belonged to one of two classes, the elect or non-elect, the number of neither of whom could, by any possibility, be either increased or diminished; and my place and destiny, as a member of one or the other of these classes, was fixed immutably from eternity. Finally, somewhere in the unrevealed future of life, if I did not die earlier, I should pass through a crisis called "concern of mind," as the result of which it would be known what destiny was, from eternity, written out for me, and "drawn by the eternal pen" in that dread volume that "lies chained to the eternal throne." All this was real to me, an object of unquestioned belief.

'Now, while such convictions of my state and destiny did, as would have been true, in the case above supposed, of necessity, exclude all consciousness of personal responsibility and desert from the sphere of religious thought, the question of my relations to these supposed eternal verities, and of my destiny in connection with the same, did press, and that very often, with awful and crushing weight upon my sensibilities. How often did the question arise, "When will the crisis in my being come? and shall I pass through it to eternal doom, or into the light of eternal day?" Then, as my mind would wander off into the great hereafter, how often

would the thought roll back upon me, with overpowering weight,"
What is my decreed destiny there?"
"Where shall I find my dwelling-place?
Shall I my everlasting days
With fiends or angels spend?"

'These infinite and eternal verities were none the less real to my mind because wholly disconnected with the ideas of moral obligation and moral desert. Hence it is that revivals of religion, periods of general religious seriousness, not unfrequently occur under ministrations, the leading doctrinal teachings of which tend but in one direction, to prevent and extinguish all proper religious convictions. Such preachers as Edwards, the Tenants, and Mr. Nettleton, were high Calvinists, but men of great revival power. Under the discourses of Edwards, for example, on such themes as, "sinners in the hands of an angry God," and, "Their feet shall slide in due time," very many of his impenitent hearers would wail aloud, and others fall helpless upon the floor. Thus aroused, they would seek and find peace in Christ. Such explanations will prepare the way for a presentation of the

'Early Religious Impressions which led to my Conversion.

'A fact which gave those aspects of religious truth which were adapted to move my sensibilities the greatest power, was my absolute conviction that all these doctrines, the most awful and impressive among them especially, were unquestionable verities. In my childhood, I had an overshadowing veneration for manhood. It appeared to me impossible that beings who knew so much could err in judgment, or could deceive. No one can conceive the shock which I received when, in growing years, the reality opened upon my mind that men and women could lie. Hence I repeated my Catechism, and listened to religious teaching at home and on the Sabbath, with an absolute and unquestioning assurance that I was hearing nothing but eternal truth.

'As soon as the idea of dying entered my mind, I had an inconceivable dread and horror of death. Wherever I was, the thought of dying, and being buried in that deep, narrow place, was seldom absent from my mind. Often, when alone, I would cry aloud for horror at the thought of death, the coffin, and the grave. In connection with such reflections, thoughts of the eternal verities that lie in the great hereafter would throw their awe-inspiring shadows over my spirits. Between my ninth and thirteenth years three events occurred, in each of which I escaped death as by a miracle. In the first instance, when wholly unable to swim, and with no one present able at all to help me, I found myself, by a momentary accident, in water far over my head. By singular presence of mind, I moved under the water toward the shore, until, in a most exhausted state, my head rose above the surface, and I was safe. Had I moved in any direction but the one I did, death would have been inevitable. The other two escapes, which were as remarkable and providential as that, I need not detail. These events brought eternity, as never before, to my apprehension. How often would I start back at the thought which would suddenly come over me that I had three times hung as by a thread over the bottomless pit, and that, had I lost my life on either occasion, eternal damnation would have been my portion! An event which made a very deep and lasting impression on my mind occurred when I was about fourteen years of age. It was the sickness and death of a school and play mate, who was very dear to me. I was one of four lads who were selected to bear that silent body, so tenderly dear to us all, into the graveyard, and set it down by the side of its low and narrow house. With what deep and impressive interest did the question often come home to my mind, "Where has the spirit gone? And what if mine, instead of his, had been called for?" As one and another dropped around me, now an aged neighbour, then a strong man or woman in middle life, then a child, and then a youth, or one just merging into manhood, how narrow the space came to appear between myself and "the undiscovered country!" I sometimes seemed to myself to be walking on a narrow path with my grave open on each side of me.

'But the influences which, more than all others, gave form and depth to my early religious impressions were what passed daily before me in the domestic circle. Very much of the religious conversation which I heard there was of an experimental character, and proceeded from the most spiritual believers in all the region round. In listening to such converse I, from time to time, got impressive insights into the interior of the Christian life. I thus became deeply impressed with the essential difference between the worldly and the Christian life, and with the opposite adaptations of each, as the soul, in one or the other state, should enter eternity.

'But what most impressed my mind was what I saw in the daily life of my mother. She was, in public regard, one of the best housekeepers known. In the morning, after the family had partaken of the meal prepared, and everything about the house was put in the most perfect order, she would take down her Bible and seat herself in her rocking-chair. How still and solemn and peaceful everything about her then appeared! No one broke the silence at such periods. After a few moments of deep thought, she would read to herself—she never read aloud then—a portion of that blessed Book which she loved so much. Then, after another season of deep and silent meditation, she would retire to some secret place for a season of prayer to God. I often listened, unknown to her, to her words, as she would open her heart to her Maker and Saviour. How often would the thought force itself in upon my mind, "O that I were possessed of the spirit that dwells in the heart of my mother!"

'Among the books which, next to her Bible, my mother loved to read, were the memoirs of the holiest men and women known in the circle of her religious faith, such as, for example, those of President and Mrs. Edwards, of the Tenants, David Brainerd, Miss Susanna Anthony, Mrs. Sarah Osborne, and Mrs. Isabella Graham. These books she commonly read aloud in my hearing, and for my benefit specially, and particularly the most impressive incidents. I have not looked into one of these books for more than half a century, yet the incidents referred to are to this day as distinctly before my mind as when I first heard them read. I refer to the wonderful manifestations of the Divine glory and love to President and Mrs. Edwards and David Brainerd. Full of interest, too, were the lives of Miss Anthony and Mrs. Osborne. In a weekly female prayer-meeting established by these holy women, and which had continued without the interruption of a single week through thirty years or more, Miss Anthony, for example, would sometimes be so borne upward in prayer for a world in sin, that she would continue on her knees for the space of one or two hours, and no one bowing with her would suspect that her prayer had been long continued. In view of "the spirit of grace and of supplications" poured out upon these women and others, President Edwards expressed the fixed belief that a period was near when revivals of religion would occur such as the world had not witnessed in ages past. Such facts made a very deep impression on my mind. Mrs. Osborne lived in widowhood to a great age, she and a granddaughter occupying a small cottage in a state of utter poverty and dependence upon the voluntary benefactions of the church and community around her. Yet she never begged a favour of any human being, and never, in a single instance, lacked her daily bread, and a full supply of it. Not unfrequently would she rise in the morning with not a particle of food in her house. "Put on the tea-kettle, daughter," the aged saint would say: "as soon as it is ready, what we need will be here;" and some one, under a Divine impression, always did come in with the very things that were wanted. In times of need, she always told her Father the facts just as they were, and never failed to obtain what she asked. When my mother would read such facts to me, and would then turn to her Bible and read such passages as, "The Lord is my Shepherd, I shall not want," how safe the people of God appeared to me under the guardianship of their Divine Shepherd, and how agonising the desire which would spring up in my mind to become a member of that sacred flock! Then the triumph and peace of those saints in the hour of death. What a parting scene was that between Mrs. Graham and her daughter at the death of the latter, which seemed to be an almost visible transfiguration! As the glorified spirit took its flight, the mother, lifting her hands, exclaimed, "I wish you much joy, my darling."

'How oft and how solemnly did I repeat that ancient utterance, "Let me die the death of the righteous, and let my last end be like his!" I never spoke in ridicule of Christians, as impenitent persons around me often did. At one time, for example, I was present when two half-brothers and several young men, all much older than myself; were disporting themselves at the expense of religion and the members of the church. I rebuked very strongly their impiety, closing with these words: "I wish that we were as well off as Christians are." All such considerations and impressions only made more visible and awful to me the "great gulph fixed" between myself and the world, on the one hand, and the people of God, on the other. Often did I express the inward wish that I had lived in the time of our Saviour, or that He were now on earth as He was eighteen hundred years ago. "Were He now here," I said, "I should know what to do. I would go right to Him, give myself wholly to His control, and trust Him to make me what He desired me to be, and He would do it." But now, what could I do, but wait for "the effectual call," were it eternally decreed for me?

'When I was about sixteen years of age, an event occurred which made an enduring impression upon my mind. I had occasion to take a quantity of grain to a mill about eight miles from home, the mill near my father's residence being stopped for repairs. While waiting for my grist, I noticed an individual with a black face, in company with a young lad, at work in a pasture near by. Having nothing else to do, I went over into the lot where they were. The supposed coloured man I found to be a white youth about two years older than myself; he having blackened his face in sport. I had been in his presence but a few moments, when I found him to be one of the most shocking blasphemers I ever met with. The chief direction of all his thoughts appeared to be to combine the most horrid oaths possible. With a kind of shuddering terror I soon left him, and returned to the mill. The miller then told me that that was the most recklessly depraved and wicked youth he had ever known. Some time before he had run away from home, had but just returned, and seemed to have but one ambition, and that was to show the community how depraved and wicked so young a person could become. About two weeks subsequently to this, I had occasion to go to that mill again. I then learned that that youth, to all appearance, was on his death-bed in his father's house a few rods distant. He had just before attended the town election at the village two miles distant, and there made himself a spectacle of terror, for reckless depravity, to all present. On his return home he was suddenly stricken down with a deadly fever. Not obtaining my grist that day, I returned for it two days after, and then and there witnessed a death scene, the memory of which never escaped me, a scene exceeding in horror anything I had ever before conceived. Like his life, the death of that youth seemed characterised by a raving madness. His aged grandfather endeavoured to speak to the dying youth about his soul. "Begone, begone, and let me alone," was the only response that could be obtained. And such wailing! After death had closed the scene, the miller, a man of God, as he returned with me to the mill, remarked that not a shadow of hope of a change for the better did that youth leave behind him. I went home from that scene a more serious, if not a better, youth. I was not, in any sense, profane or immoral, like that youth; yet, like him, I was, as I well knew, in the accepted sense of the term, a sinner under condemnation to eternal death. No one who has not had similar experience, can conceive the fearful terror often awakened in my mind at the thought of dying in sin. Such impressions were deepened by a remark which a neighbour—the profanest man I ever knew—made about that time to the deacon of our church. The latter had occasion, one hot summer's day, to call upon this man. Finding him hoeing corn, and perceiving that the row he was on terminated at the road where the deacon was standing, the latter waited until the man came up. Having finished his row, the poor man threw down his hoe, and wiping the dripping perspiration from his face, exclaimed, "Deacon Branch, is not this hard—to be obliged to toil like a slave all one's life, and go to hell at last? Tell me, is not this hard?" "Yes," the thought often passed through my mind, "to go to hell at last, that is the end of a life of sin! Will my life thus terminate?"

'About this time reports of revivals of religion of wonderful power in various parts of the country reached us, particularly in the eastern States under Mr. Nettleton and others; and the impression came over me that I should soon be in the midst of such an ingathering. I then began to hear the words repeated, "The one shall be taken, and the other left." With what impressiveness did the question often present itself, "Shall I be among the happy number that shall be taken, or among the non-elect who shall be left to die in their sins?"

'Such were the religious impressions to which I was subject prior to my conversion, and which were preparatory to that event; impressions which became deeper, and more and more frequent, as I grew in years. And what was the result upon my life and character? This is a very important inquiry. Many would naturally infer, that I was "not far from the kingdom of God." Instead of this, aside from the fact that I was chargeable with no form of immorality, vice, or crime, I sincerely doubt whether there was, in all the world, a more godless youth than I was. After I had ceased to offer the Lord's Prayer at my mother's knee, I had never uttered a word or sentence in prayer to God. I had never, even in thought, thanked Him for a blessing received, or confessed or asked forgiveness for a single sin, or sought a favour at the hands of my Maker. I had never raised the question, even in thought, as to whether what I did, or neglected to do, was pleasing or displeasing to Him, or made the thought of pleasing or displeasing Him a motive for any act I had put forth, or refrained from putting forth. Nor had I ever raised the inquiry, "What shall I do to be saved?" or exercised a thought or put forth an act relatively to that end, or made the deep religious impressions to which I was so often subject a motive for any such thought or act. Nor did the conviction ever, for a moment, have place in my mind, that my interior or outer life *ought,* in any respect, to be, or to have been, different from what it was. No religious impression to which I was subject ever induced in my mind anything approaching the conviction of duty, obligation, or moral desert. My conscience, as far as any such convictions are concerned, was, as I have before said, as dead within me as if it had not existed at all. A thick and impenetrable veil was ever before my mind, rendering the entrance of such convictions impossible. How, it may be asked, was such a life possible? If we should recur to the religious teachings with which my mind was saturated during all those years, the question is answered at once. According to what is absolutely affirmed in the Confession of Faith and the Catechisms, and what I absolutely believed, the following immutable facts were true of me in my unregenerate state; I having had no choice or agency whatever in inducing the state under consideration. I. It was utterly impossible for me to will or to do anything right or good, and not to will and do what is sinful, or to will or do anything to procure any Divine influence enabling me to refuse the evil and choose the good. 2. It was absolutely impossible for me to accept the offers of grace in the Gospel, until after I was "quickened and renewed by the Holy Ghost," a change in which I was "altogether passive." 3. The number of those who were to be thus "effectually called," was from eternity so fixed and predetermined that it could by no possibility be "either increased or diminished." Granting all this to be true, why should I attempt to will or do the good, or not to will or do the evil, when the attempt itself would be nothing but sin? Why should I pray, when the service itself would be in the sight of God nothing but an abomination? How could the conviction have place in my conscience, that I *ought* to perform a revealed and recognised impossibility? Granting these doctrines to be true, we can no more conceive that unregenerate man, until God, in the exercise of His sovereignty, has made him the subject of "effectual calling," can be under any obligation to become holy, than we can conceive of the annihilation of space, or of an event without a cause.'

It will be seen that our author did not change his views on this subject from the time he first gave the below Lectures to the time of his Autobiography thirty years later. We commend therefore this work, along with his similar work on the *Doctrine of the Will*, written a few years prior, to the public as his mature mind on the important subjects of moral government, obligation, and the Christian religion.

This Treaties, along with all of his latter works written in England, was given with English spelling; and we have retained the original as with all our publications of these authors. The only differences are in the printed format and the correction of occasional typos.

RICHARD M. FRIEDRICH
GRAND RAPIDS, 27 th, *March*, 2002.

INTRODUCTORY PREFACE.

THE reasons which have induced me, a stranger in England, and coming into this kingdom with no expectation whatever of publishing any new work while remaining here, to present the following production to the British public, are these. Some time prior to leaving my native country, I remarked to one of my associates in the Institution over which I am permitted to preside, that I was perfectly certain that the common explanation of the ninth of Romans was based upon a fundamental misapprehension of the apostle's meaning and design in the chapter; and that, if my life was spared, I would attempt, at least, a demonstration of the fact, by giving the true exposition. I had at that time satisfied my own mind, in respect to what was the design of the apostle in the chapter, and in respect to the meaning of all the particular passages found in it, with one or two exceptions; and I left home with the intention of devoting a large portion of the present winter, wherever I might be called to spend it, in a more extended and critical study of the chapter than I had before been able to give it.

On my arrival in this kingdom, I learned with much interest that a new work on this very chapter had just appeared from the pen of the Rev. James Morison, of Kilmarnock, Scotland. On giving this work, consisting of upwards of five hundred pages, a very careful perusal, I was not a little interested to find that the author had fixed upon the identical passage that I had done, as presenting the key to the true explanation of the whole chapter, and that he had traversed this important portion of inspiration on the same line on which I was myself threading my way through it. In respect to the production of Mr. Morison, permit me to express the opinion, that it is one of the lasting monuments of biblical criticism of this century, and that it will never be answered by an appeal to the universally admitted laws of sound interpretation. In the perusal of this work my own ideal of the apostle's meaning and design, throughout the entire chapter, matured into a full consummation. In developing this ideal to my esteemed friend and brother in Christ, Rev. John Stevenson, he urged upon me the preparation and public delivery, and final publication, if, after the delivery, it should be thought expedient, of the present course of lectures. They were accordingly prepared and delivered, and, in conformity with the desire of many who heard, them, they are now presented to the public, and commended to the candid investigation of all honest inquirers of "the truth as it is in Jesus." Such are the circumstances which have led to the publication of this work during my present sojourn in this kingdom.

The considerations which have induced me to reject the common, and especially high Calvinist, explanations of this chapter, are the following: 1. A remark of the celebrated biblical scholar, Rev. Moses Stuart, made to the class of which I was a member, when a pupil of his, that the cases of Isaac, Esau, and Jacob, together with the sayings to Moses and Pharaoh, found in the chapter, were simply illustrations of some proposition which the apostle was aiming to establish and elucidate, and of course should be explained accordingly. This remark started the fundamental inquiry in my mind, What is this proposition? and how are these cases to be explained so as to elucidate and confirm it? In pushing my inquiries in this direction, I early saw that the high Calvinistic explanation was not based, as every true one must be, upon a clear ascertainment of this proposition, and that the examples under consideration were not, in fact, so explained as to elucidate and confirm it. Hence the conviction forced itself upon my mind, that there must be something fundamentally wrong in the explanation,—an explanation which presented the chapter as constituted of masses of broken fragments, instead of possessing, as all Paul's reasonings do, a beautiful harmony and logical consistency throughout. 2. I saw that this explanation rested entirely upon a total misapprehension of an historical fact, of which, if we will inquire, we cannot be mistaken, to wit, the assumption that Paul is reasoning in this chapter as a predestinarian, against the Jew as an anti-predestinarian. Now the facts are the direct opposite of this. Every solitary sect among the Jews, with the exception of the Sadducees, —a small sect to which Paul never refers in his reasonings, —were, as a plain matter of fact, high predestinarians, and could never have been at issue with Paul as a predestinarian. I hence saw clearly that an explanation which rested upon such an assumption, and which could not be true if that assumption was false, as I could not but know that this was, could not possibly be the true exposition. 3. I saw that this exposition presented the different portions of the chapter in the most unnatural relations to each other conceivable. Paul, for example, commences the chapter by affirming, in the most solemn manner conceivable, his "great heaviness and continual sorrow of heart" in view of the impending doom of the Jew; and then, according to this exposition, goes directly on to show that this doom accords with and results from an eternal decree and purpose of God. No exposition can possibly place the different portions of the chapter in relations to each other more unnatural and repugnant. Whenever a devout and sanctified mind contemplates any event as an object of an eternal decree of God, it is then to such mind an object of acquiescence and submission, and not of sorrow and anguish of heart; and any exposition which presents such an event as the opposite of this, as the one under consideration does, the doom of the Jews, cannot be the true one. 4. This exposition, as I saw most clearly, made the apostle palpably contradict himself in different parts of the chapter. In the first instance, he presents the doom of his countrymen as resulting from an eternal decree of God, and then, at the close of the chapter, represents this same event as resulting wholly from another and different cause, "seeking salvation not by faith, but as it were by deeds of law." I could not but be assured that an exposition, which made an inspired writer thus palpably contradict himself, cannot be the true exposition. 5. I saw clearly that there was an exposition which most manifestly accorded with the real design of the apostle in the chapter, and which gave to all its parts a beautiful harmony and consistency throughout. Such were some of the considerations which led me first to doubt the common exposition of this chapter, and finally to adopt that given in these lectures. The question whether the true exposition has been attained, is now left with the candid public to decide.

There is an impression upon the minds of individuals, holding views the opposite of those advocated in the following lectures, which demands a passing notice, in this connection. The impression to which I refer is this: that these views are held not at all from respect to the teachings of inspiration, but as the exclusive result of a certain system of mental philosophy; and that the plain language of the Bible has been perverted, to meet the exigencies of such system. Individuals who adduce such objections are undoubtedly very sincere in the impression that they themselves are wholly free from the influence of pre-formed philosophical systems in the study of the Scriptures. They are wholly influenced, they judge, in the formation of their theological opinions, by respect for the Word of God. Now, if this class of individuals could only see themselves as others see them, they might, perhaps, entertain opinions of themselves, as Bible students, quite different from what they now do. Suppose that every person who is at all influenced, in his explanations of particular passages, by pre-formed systems of mental philosophy, were to receive from God the impression of certain peculiar features of countenance, indicative of this fact. Who of us might not be filled with self-astonishment, the next time we beheld ourselves in the glass? Suppose that, in the case of the individuals adducing the objection under consideration, there could be a total oblivion of all systems of mental philosophy, of all pre-formed theories of human depravity; and that they should approach the Scriptures as the exclusive pupils of the Spirit, to interpret the sacred text in sacred conformity to the laws of interpretation. How do they know but that the Bible would be a very different book to them from what it now is?

They meet, for example, with such passages as the following:—"And you hath he quickened who were dead in trespasses and sins." To them it appears quite manifest that such a passage does and must teach, 1. That all men unrenewed by grace are not only under condemnation on account of trespasses and sins, but that they are in a state of total disability to all good; and, 2. That in regeneration, men are not the free, active subjects of a divine influence, "purifying themselves by obeying the truth through the Spirit" that is, by yielding to the truth presented to their minds by the Spirit, but the passive recipients of a divine resistless energy producing in them a new and holy nature. All who explain the passage as not teaching these dogmas are regarded as "spoiled through philosophy and vain deceit, after the traditions of men, and not after Christ." But what is it, friend, that makes it so perfectly manifest to your mind that this passage does and must teach these peculiar dogmas? What but a certain pre-formed theory of depravity and regeneration? That this passage teaches the *fact* that men are "dead in (on account of) trespasses and sins," and that, in regeneration, they are quickened from death to life by a divine influence, there is no diversity of opinion among evangelical Christians. The difference pertains exclusively to the *form*, and not to the *fact*, of the death and quickening referred to. Of the *fact* we are here clearly informed, and hence no difference of opinion exists in respect to it. Of the *form*, we are not at all informed in this passage, and here, consequently, a difference of opinion obtains. Any person that infers, from this passage, not the *fact*, but a certain *form* of death and quickening, is wholly influenced, in such inferences, not by what the passage itself teaches, but by a pre-formed theory of depravity and regeneration. Of this death, whatever its nature may be, one thing is quite certain, that in it men are not passive, but active. "Wherein (in which state of death) ye walked," (were active agents.) Now, if men are active in this state, how do we know, as far as anything asserted in this passage is concerned, but that the nature of that activity is such, as implies the ability to the opposite form of activity? If men are indeed, as we are here taught that they are, active in this state, how do we know, from anything found in this passage, but that, in the divine quickening here referred to, they pass, under a divine influence, freely and voluntarily, from one form of voluntary activity to its opposite? Take away all pre-formed theories of depravity and regeneration, and nothing found in this passage will even *appear* to teach either this or the opposite doctrine; the exclusive object of the passage being to affirm the fact of man's death by nature "in trespasses and sins," and of his regeneration by a divine quickening, and not at all the *nature* or *form* of either.

So, where the individuals referred to meet with the declaration, "Ye are his workmanship, created in Christ Jesus unto good works," how manifest it appears to them that the doctrine of the sinner's passivity in regeneration is here most undeniably taught; and that no person can hold the opposite doctrine, excepting through the influence of philosophical speculations. Suppose, now, that, as simple pupils of the Spirit, we leave this passage for a few moments, and inquire elsewhere in the divine word for some direct and positive teachings, if any there are, in respect to the agencies and influences actually combined in regeneration. We shall find that they are three: the Spirit presenting the truth to the mind; the truth thus presented operating upon the mind, to "convince of sin, of righteousness, and of judgment;" the sinner voluntarily yielding to the truth as thus presented. Thus we read, in different places, that men, in regeneration, are "born of God," "born of the Spirit;" and again, that they are "born again *by* the word (truth) of God;" and, finally, that in this very change the creature "purifies himself by obeying the truth through the Spirit," (yielding to the truth presented to his mind by the Spirit.) Thus, as the exclusive pupils of the Bible, we learn that in regeneration, in "passing from death unto life," men are not the passive recipients of a divine energy, but that, under the influence of the truth and Spirit of God, they voluntarily pass from one form of activity to another of a different and opposite character. Thus divinely enlightened, suppose we return to the passage above cited. What is there in this passage that contradicts the divine teachings which we have elsewhere found on the subject of regeneration? For aught that appears in the passage, itself, the "workmanship," and "creation," here referred to, may be not the formation of a new *nature* or *constitution*, but of a new *character,* a voluntary change from one form of activity to another, a change induced by the truth and Spirit of God. Nothing but a pre-formed philosophical theory pertaining to the nature of human depravity and regeneration, can make any such passage even *appear* to teach, not the *fact* of a divine workmanship, and creation in regeneration, but the form thereof. "Happy is he that condemneth not another in that which he alloweth."

It is not at all unlikely, that the views presented in these lectures on the influences of the Spirit, will be very honestly attributed by not a few to a certain system of mental philosophy; while the objectors will as honestly suppose, that their own theory of the Spirit's influences were formed from exclusive respect to divine teachings on this subject. If there is anything that deserves to be denominated the theological hobby of England, I hazard but little in saying that it is this,—that in almost every discourse, the sinner must be told of his dependence for regeneration upon the Spirit, and then exhorted to pray for his converting influences. Whence did this peculiar mode of teaching have its origin? Do we find anything like it in the Bible? No such form of teaching can be found there; nothing which even looks in that direction. Where are sinners, whether careless in their sins, or inquiring "what shall we do to be saved," counselled, exhorted, or commanded, not to "repent and believe on the Lord Jesus Christ," but to pray for the converting influences of the Spirit? Whence did or could such a mode of teaching, one so unlike and opposite to all scriptural example, have its origin, but in a certain philosophical theory pertaining to regeneration? Ought not good and wise men to put the inquiry, whether a theory which has led them in a direction so manifestly opposite to all the forms of divine teaching and example on the subject, is not itself contrary to "the law and the testimony?"

In the following Lectures, the reader will perceive, I trust, that it has been the object of the speaker to *"reason* out of the Scriptures," and not to denounce those who dissent from his views. May he not hope, that in a similar spirit his work may be met, even by those who differ from him in opinion?

London, January 17*th,* 1850.

EXPOSITION OF ROMANS IX., ETC.

LECTURE I.

Verses 1—18.

PRELIMINARY OBSERVATIONS.

1. There are two epistles of Paul which have a direct and special reference to the Jews—the Epistle to the Romans, and the Epistle to the Hebrews. The first appears under the name of the apostle. The second, though written by him, is anonymous. The question might arise, why did Paul take this particular course in addressing his countrymen? The reasons are obvious. Had he addressed the Jews directly, and in his own name, such were their prejudices against him, that they would never have read his epistles at all. By arguing the question in difference between him and them before the church of Rome, and by addressing them anonymously, however, he had some hope of gaining a hearing. When an individual speaks of us to a third person, and especially to a distant community in whom we are deeply interested, we naturally feel a great curiosity to know what he has said of us. Paul, then, manifested great wisdom in arguing the point in difference between the Jew and the Christian before the church and people of Rome, the capital of the empire to which all were alike subject, in the first instance; and in addressing an anonymous epistle to his brethren, in the second. Their curiosity would be greatly excited to understand what was written about them in the former epistle, and the truth would thus be brought distinctly before their minds through its instrumentality; and existing prejudices against him, as an individual, would, as far as possible, be avoided in

the case of the latter. There were many Jewish Christians in Rome also, that needed to be instructed in the way of God more perfectly, and to be confirmed in the faith, by having all their remaining tendencies to Judaism fully corrected. Gentile converts, also, not only in Rome, but everywhere else, and in all ages, who should read the epistle, would better understand the way of life, by seeing the plan of redemption by Christ, and through faith in Him, placed in full and distinct contrast with a system of error, with which, in many minds, it was likely to be confounded. Such, as I suppose, are some of Paul's reasons for the method adopted in the two epistles under consideration.

2. Of the Epistle to the Romans, the first eleven chapters, after certain introductory remarks, are wholly occupied in arguing three great questions in difference between the Christian and the Jew; the questions pertaining to the doctrine of Justification, of Sanctification, and the privileges to which the Jew fancied himself entitled consequent on his relations to Abraham, and the other patriarchs, Isaac and Jacob. The doctrine of Justification, he argues and elucidates in the first five chapters. The discussion of that of Sanctification occupies the next three chapters; and the elucidation of the relations of the Jew to Abraham, and his privileges consequent thereon, occupies the remaining three. The argument of the apostle throughout is made to bear directly and immediately upon, and to confirm, the proposition which he lays down in chapter i., ver. 16, 17. "For I am not ashamed of the gospel of Christ; for it is the power of God unto salvation to every one that believeth; to the Jew first, and also to the Greek. For therein is the righteousness of God revealed from faith to faith; as it is written, The just shall live by faith." The real meaning of these verses may be thus expressed. I am not ashamed to proclaim anywhere in the wide world the gospel of Christ, and this is the reason why I am not ashamed to do so. This gospel contains in itself a divine power, all-efficacious to the complete salvation of every one that receives it by faith. For

in it God's righteousness or plan of salvation is revealed, to wit:—righteousness or salvation "from," that is, by faith, and revealed "to faith," that is, for the purpose of being received by faith by all who hear it. Moreover, this doctrine of righteousness or salvation by faith accords with the express teachings of Scripture. "As it is written, the just shall live," or obtain righteousness or salvation, "by faith." The apostle then proceeds to elucidate and confirm this fundamental doctrine of salvation by faith, by placing it in opposition to the three great errors of the Jew above referred to. By showing, in respect to each form of error, that the doctrine of the Jew must be false, and the Christian doctrine true, he elucidates and confirms the great fundamental article of Christianity, the doctrine of salvation by faith, in distinction from, and in opposition to, every other system.

3. The ninth, with the two following chapters, is, as I said, occupied with the elucidation of the doctrine of righteousness by faith, in opposition to the error of the Jew, founded on his relations to Abraham. As preparatory to the attainment of the object I have in view in these lectures, special attention is now invited to the error under consideration. The Jew supposed that, as a descendant of Abraham, he could not by any possibility be lost, unless he openly apostatized from his religion, or became guilty of the most flagrant forms of crime. When entreated to repent, or accept of mercy, and especially to consent to receive it through Christ, he repelled the exhortation with contempt and indignation. "He had Abraham to his father." He need not exercise either "repentance towards God, or faith towards Christ." As a descendant of Abraham, and in consequence of that descent, his salvation was secure, his perdition impossible. Christ, therefore, was "to the Jew a stumbling-block." With what earnestness did John the Baptist guard his hearers against the common error of his nation. To this error the Christian fathers refer in their controversies with the Jews. "Ye," (Jews,) says Justin Martyr, "expect to be saved, since ye are the lineally descended children of Jacob." Again, he says, "Your

Rabbins deceive both themselves and you, supposing that the everlasting kingdom shall assuredly be given to them who are lineally descended from Abraham, even although they be sinners and unbelievers, and disobedient toward God." "All Israel shall have a share in the world to come," says the Talmud, the great national work of the Jews. Says one of their writers about the beginning of the Christian era, "Because of the works of our righteous fathers, who were of old, we shall be redeemed." It was this delusion which made Christ a stumbling-block to the Jew. How important, then, would the apostle deem it, as a means of bringing him to Christ, to wrest this delusion from his mind! Under the influence of this, and the two fundamental errors discussed in the first eight chapters of this epistle, Paul saw, that the masses of his own countrymen were about to reject God's righteousness, which is through and obtained only by faith, and, in consequence of that rejection, to be given over of God to hopeless reprobation. Under the pressure of this awful fact, the apostle opens the discussion of the relation of the Jews to Abraham and the patriarchs in the chapter before us.

4. Connected with the error of the Jew in respect to himself, consequent on his ideas of the efficacy of observing the ceremonial law, and of his relations to Abraham, was another error, equally fundamental, pertaining to the Gentiles. He not only held that he was elected of God to eternal life, simply and exclusively on these grounds, but, also, that *they*, unless they became circumcised and united with the Jews by being adopted into their nation, were, whatever their moral character might be, hopelessly reprobated of God. God was the God of the Jews only, and in no case the God of the Gentiles remaining out of the pale of the Jewish community. This error of the Jew the apostle refutes, in connection with the others above referred to. We must keep all these facts in mind, in reading the Epistle to the Romans, or else we shall not appreciate the apostle's reasonings. In respect to the statements above made, there is

a general, if not universal, agreement among evangelical commentators on the Scriptures. None, probably, would deny any of them. The difference of opinion between them pertains, not to the general plan or design of the epistle, but to the special explanation of particular passages, and especially of the chapter which we are now to consider. One of the most common errors, as it appears to me, of commentators, in the explanation of particular passages, lies here: that they forget the real relations of all such passages to the *general* design referred to, and consequently fail to explain them in the light of it.

5. The reason why the apostle commences the chapter with the most solemn asseveration of concern for and love to his own brethren, the Jews, is obvious. When we expose the errors and delusions of others, we very commonly appeal to them as enemies; so the apostle appeared to his countrymen. Hence, his solemn asservations of his real feelings towards them, and of his reasons for all that he had written and spoken concerning them.

Explanation of Verses 1—5.

We advance now to a direct consideration of the portion of the chapter before us, the portion to which attention is to be directed in this lecture. I will first direct attention to the first five verses.

"I say the truth in Christ. I lie not, my conscience also bearing me witness in the holy Ghost. For I could wish that myself were accursed from Christ for my brethren, or my kinsmen according to the flesh who are Israelites: to whom pertaineth the adoption, and the glory, and the covenants, and the giving of the law, and the service of God, and the promises: whose are the fathers, and of whom, as concerning the flesh, Christ came, who is over all, God blessed forever. Amen."

In respect to these verses, also, there is a very general agreement among commentators, excepting in reference to one or two clauses; and in respect to these, the difference has no reference whatever to anything bearing particularly upon our general inquiries. The passage naturally divides itself into four parts: the affirmation, including verse 1, "I say the truth," &c.; the thing affirmed, verse 2, "That I have great heaviness;" the object of this sorrow, verse 3, "My brethren:" and certain circumstances connected with their state, which aggravated this sorrow, verses 4, 5, "Who are Israelites." The phrase, "I could wish that myself," &c., is admitted by all to be a parenthesis, and may be considered by itself.

We will first consider the asseveration. Two explanations have been given of the words "in Christ." They have been considered as a part of the formula of an oath. The passage would then read, "I say the truth *by* Christ." It is enough to say, in reply to this explanation, that wherever the words *in Christ* have this meaning, they are found in conjunction with a verb of swearing, one necessarily implying an oath. Such an explanation, then, should not be given to them in this connection. The second form of explanation is this: these words may be connected with the pronoun "I." The passage would then read thus: "*I in Christ,*"—that is, in the consciousness of my union with Christ,—"speak the truth, I lie not." In other words, what I am about to affirm, I declare, in the consciousness of my union with Christ, to be the truth, and nothing false. The term "conscience," in the following clause, should be understood as synonymous with *consciousness.* In this sense the term is often used in the Bible. The words, *in the Holy Ghost,* are, of course, to be explained in the same manner as the words, *in Christ,* have been. The meaning of the whole verse may be thus expressed: In the consciousness of my union with Christ I speak, or am about to speak, the truth; I lie not; my own consciousness, while I am under the influence of the Holy Ghost, testifying to my integrity in what I am about to utter. Some connect the words, the Holy Ghost, with the phrase, I lie not, and make the following clause parenthetic. No difference in regard to the real meaning of the passage is made, whichever way it is explained.

The thing affirmed is found in verse 2:—"That I have great heaviness and continual sorrow in my heart." The term *heaviness* designates the idea of excessive grief. When an object excites great pain to us whenever we think of it, it is said to be to us a source of *continual* sorrow. So Paul asserts, that he experienced the most excessive grief, and continual sorrow to his heart.

But who, or what, is the object of this sorrow? This we are informed of in the following verse: "for my brethren, my kinsmen according to the flesh." The explanation of the parenthetic clause, "I could wish," &c., I shall omit till I have explained the two following verses. The meaning of the verses which we have now considered may be thus expressed. In the consciousness of my union with Christ I speak the truth; I lie not; my own consciousness, while I am speaking under the direct illumination and influence of the Holy Ghost, bearing testimony to my integrity, when I affirm that I have the most excessive grief and continual sorrow in my heart for my brethren, my kinsmen according to the flesh.

In the two following verses, the apostle points out certain circumstances connected with his brethren and kinsmen, by which his heaviness and sorrow of heart were aggravated. 1. They were Israelites, that is, descendants from Israel, and consequently, from the patriarch Abraham, and Isaac through him. 2. To them pertained the adoption, that is, the peculiar privilege of being adopted of God, as his peculiar people. Thus we read, Deut. vii. 6: "For thou *art* an holy people unto the LORD thy God; the LORD thy God hath chosen thee to be a special people unto himself, above all people that *are* upon the face of the earth." No other nation had been thus adopted of God. 3. To the Jewish nation also, and to them only, pertained *the glory*,—that is, the visible symbol of the divine presence which attended them from Egypt, and finally rested over the ark of the covenant in the first temple. This visible manifestation of God was called the shekinah of the Jews. 4. Another special privilege of the Israelites, was the covenants, that is, the various compacts or promises to the patriarch, and the nation itself, of the divine protection and favor. 5. Another peculiarity of the Israelites pertained to the "giving of the law," that is, in the language of Mr. Morison, "to the sublime and glorious publication of the moral law upon Mount Sinai, when God pronounced, in the audience of the people, the ten cardinal commandments, and subsequently delivered them to Moses, engraved on two tables of stone." No nation or people had been thus distinguished of God. So we read, (Dent. v. 6,) "For who *is there of* all flesh, that hath heard the voice of the living God speaking out of the midst of the fire, as we *have,* and lived?" 6. Still another peculiarity of the Israelites was, that to them pertained *the service of God,*—that is, the sublime ritual service which God prescribed for them. The words, *of God,* are not in the original. The term *service* only is found there. 7. Another peculiarity still of the Jews, was *the promises,*—that is, of the Messiah, and of the spread of the gospel of peace and salvation through them to all the nations of the earth. 8. In the commencement of verse 5, we have another peculiarity of the Jews: "*Whose are the fathers,*"—that is, they are the descendants of the great patriarchs, Abraham, Isaac, and Jacob. No nation on earth could boast of such an ancestry, an ancestry so great, so wise, so good, and so favored of God. 9. But the *great* peculiarity still remains to be mentioned. They were the *messianic people,* "of whom as concerning the flesh Christ came, who is over all, God blessed forever. Amen." The two-fold nature of Christ, the physical and spiritual, the human and divine, are here brought distinctly and undeniably to view. In respect to the former. Christ was of the Jews, one of their brethren, "bone of their bone, and flesh of their flesh." In respect to the latter, He is over all; God, that is the Supreme God, who should be blessed by all creatures forever and ever. "Amen,"—that is, so let it be; or, thus let him be blessed. Such were the peculiarities of the Jews. Such were the circumstances which added to the poignancy of Paul's grief in respect to them.

We will now consider the meaning of the clause in verse 3:—"I could wish that myself," &c. To be "accursed from Christ," means, according to the literal and necessary signification of the words, to be forever separated from Christ, in a state of hopeless accursedness. When an individual seeks that which is necessarily connected with such a state as separation from Christ, he is said, in Scripture, to seek the state itself. Thus it is said. (Prov. viii. 36,) "they that hate me" (wisdom or religion) "love death." The words, "I could wish," do not express the true meaning of the original. The verb rendered *could wish*, is in the imperfect tense, the tense that refers to past time, and of course relates to a state of mind in which Paul had been, and not to that in which he then was. The real meaning of the phrase may be thus expressed:—I was myself once in a state of mind in which I *did* wish to be eternally separated from Christ, and, in this sense, willed my own hopeless accursedness. Why did Paul use this language here? He was writing about his brethren, who were then in the very state of mind, relatively to Christ, in which he had been. Then they were, and to this day are, accustomed to pronounce Jesus accursed. As we can be saved only by becoming united to Him by faith, to will a separation from Him is equivalent to willing our own damnation. The meaning of Paul, then, is this:—I know the condition of my brethren. They wish themselves accursed from Christ. I once—oh, horrid wish!—willed myself to be thus accursed. How can I but feel for my brethren, who are now in the state in which I once was?—a state which I tremble even to think of. This is the explanation of the phrase given by Mr. Morison, and is the only one that to my mind is perfectly, and, in all respects, satisfactory.

The apostle has now affirmed his sorrow of heart, the objects of that sorrow, his brethren the Jews, and the circumstances connected with them which imparted such fearful poignancy to his grief in respect to them, to wit, the fact of his once having been himself in their precise condition; their descent from such God-fearing and God-obedient and believing ancestors, and the privileges which pertained to them as thus descended. But what the circumstances were, connected with the Jews, which were the source and cause of this sorrow, the apostle has not told us. That he has left us to infer for ourselves, the cause and source being so obvious that he had no occasion to specify them. It was, as all commentators will agree, the melancholy fact, that such a people, instead of walking in the footsteps of their godly ancestors, and availing themselves of the great salvation proffered to them through Christ, were about, in consequence of rejecting that salvation, to be delivered over to hopeless reprobacy, and were about to incur that reprobation under the fearful delusion that their relations to the patriarchs and consequent privileges, instead of increasing their obligations to be holy themselves, actually shielded them from the curse of God, whatever their personal character should be, and rendered faith in Christ unnecessary.

Such, as all admit, was the cause of the apostle's grief in respect to the Jews. Under such circumstances, and pressed down with such feelings and apprehensions, which course would he be most likely to take in his subsequent reasonings? Would he proceed to show that the unbelief and reprobation of the Jew were the object of an eternal, immutable, and all-necessitating decree—an event which he could by no possibility avoid? Would he not rather attempt to erase this fearful delusion from his mind, and thus, if possible, prevent his destruction? We now advance to the inquiry, which of these two courses the apostle actually did take.

The true answer to these questions turns wholly upon the explanation to be given to the first sentence in verse 6 to which very special attention is now invited. The sentence is this—"Not as though the word of God had taken none effect." The term "*for*" in the next sentence connects all that follows in the whole chapter with, makes it depend upon, this one sentence. As to this statement there is, I believe, a perfect agreement among commentators, and the case is so obvious that there hardly can be a disagreement on this point. The question is, What is the real, meaning of this sentence?

Here permit me, in the first place, to call special attention to an important particle which is found in the original Greek, but which has been wholly omitted in the authorized version, and as wholly overlooked by all commentators with whom I am acquainted excepting Mr. Morison.[3] It is the particle *de,* which, in such connections as that in which it is here found, is always translated but, or by some term equivalent to it in its meaning. This term, when located as it is here, has a fixed and definite meaning in the Greek. It

---

[3] "There is," says Mr. Morison, "a little but not insignificant word which our translators have neglected to render. It is a very common particle in all Greek writings, and it occurs many hundreds of times in the New Testament. It has very frequently an 'adversative,' or, stronger still, an 'oppositive' meaning, and then it is generally translated 'but.' In this same epistle, for example, it occurs in chap. ii. 10. 'Tribulation and anguish upon every, soul of man that doeth evil, of the Jew first and also of the Gentile; *but* glory, honor, and peace, to every one that doeth good, to the Jew first, and also to the Gentile.' It occurs again in chap. vi. 23—'For the wages of sin is death, *but* the gift of God is eternal life through Jesus Christ our Lord.' Now it ought to have had, in the passage before us, the same rendering. When it is employed in the manner in which it is used in this clause, it is never redundant. The very first word, then, of the sixth verse should have been 'but;' 'But not as though the word of God had taken none effect.'"

separates words, clauses, and sentences, where one is opposed to the other, and where what is affirmed in one is denied in the other. Thus we may say, in English, of an individual, he is a talented, *but* not a good, a good, *but* not a prudent man. This term, then, connects this sentence by way of opposition with what goes before, and makes the apostle deny of the Jew what is expressed *in the sentence,* as not implied in what he had previously affirmed of him. The meaning of the sentence may be thus expressed. But it is not with the Jew, in consequence of relations to the patriarchs, &c., as though the word of God had taken none effect.

But what are we to understand by the clause the "word of God," in this connection? The phrase, the word of God, has, among others, three distinct meanings in different passages in the Bible. 1. Any declaration of God. 2. Some divine promise. 3. A divine threatening. In the sense last named, the phrase is used in such passages as Heb. iv. 12. "The word (threatening) of God is quick and powerful." In a similar sense the term word, translated "work," is used in the 28th verse of Romans, ch. 9. "He will finish the work (word) and cut it short in righteousness; because a short work (word) will the Lord make upon the earth." That is, He will speedily execute his word of threatening, and cut it short in righteousness, ("execute it speedily in righteous vengeance,") because he will cause his word of threatening to be executed upon the earth. That the phrase, "*the word of God,*" is used in this sense in the passage under consideration, is perfectly evident from the following considerations. 1. These words are as well adapted to express this idea as any other, and may as properly, as far as usage is concerned, be employed in this sense, as in either of the others named above. This statement no one at all acquainted with the Greek language will deny. The real meaning to be attached to such words must in all instances, be learned from the context. 2. The divine threatenings at *that* time hanging over the Jew,—threatenings under which he was about to fall, but from which he vainly supposed himself, consequent on his patriarchal descent, secure,—are the special objects of the apostle's attention, in the verses preceding. These threatenings, and the relations of his countrymen to them, were the exclusive source of the excessive sorrow referred to. God's word of threatening, and not of promise, was the object of special attention. All the laws of correct interpretation require us to suppose the former, and not the latter, to be referred to in the phrase, "the word of God," in this passage. 3. According to this construction, the apostle directly and immediately denies the great error of the Jew, based upon the very circumstances previously specified. The Jew did, in fact, suppose himself, in consequence of the relations and privileges referred to, free from all exposure to God's word of threatening denounced against the wicked. We ought then to put that construction here upon the words under consideration, which will make the apostle deny that error. 4. Everything said in the entire chapter most readily, as we shall see hereafter, falls in with this construction. 5. In this very sense the term "word" is, as we have seen above, used in a subsequent part of this chapter. 6. The passages of Scripture cited in a subsequent part of this chapter, to prove the proposition containing these words, are threatenings, and not promises. See verses 26—29. These passages are all cited expressly to confirm the facts and arguments adduced by the apostle to establish this one proposition; and, as the passages themselves are threatenings, in the same light should we understand the phrase "the word of God," in the verse before us. 7. It is this very error of the Jew, to wit, that he was not exposed to the threatened judgments of God against the wicked that the apostle denies in the remaining part of the verse, and proceeds to overthrow in his subsequent reasonings. "For they are not all Israel that are of Israel," &c. The Jew affirmed that "all who were Israel (his natural descendants) were Israel," that is, his spiritual as well as natural offspring, and consequently heirs with him of eternal life, and free from all exposure to God's word of threatening. This is what the apostle denies. It is to God's word of threatening, and not to his word of promise, as commentators generally though not universally suppose, that the apostle refers in the sentence, "Not as though the word of God had taken none effect."

The phrase "hath taken none effect," is a single word in the original. Its meaning is, according to the best Lexicons, to fall out of, to fall from or off; to fall from any former state or condition, to become inefficacious or vain. Its meaning in this place evidently is, to cease to be efficacious, or to lose its former power. The meaning of the whole sentence, then, may be thus expressed. The case of the Jew consequent on his relations and privileges as a descendant of the ancient patriarchs, great and important as these privileges are, is not such that the word of God's threatening has ceased to be efficacious, or lost its curse-inflicting power in respect to him, should he continue in sin, and reject the mercy of God in Christ.

This is the proposition that the apostle now proceeds to prove and elucidate. How has he done this? Can you suppose that he has attempted to prove such proposition, by showing that a portion of the nation were eternally and unconditionally elected to salvation, and a portion in a similar manner reprobated to eternal death? What tendency is there in such a dogma to impress an individual with the conviction that if he should reject God's righteousness, nothing could shield him from the curse of God? Would not the apostle rather proceed to prove, as I will now attempt to show that he does, that relationship to Abraham and the patriarchs does not render the rejecter of mercy secure against the curse of God? The proposition, then, which the apostle proceeds to establish and elucidate, is this. The case of the Jew, notwithstanding his patriarchal descent, does not render God's word of threatening inefficacious in regard to him any more than in regard to other sinners. In accomplishing this object, he first makes an affirmation containing the reason why descent from the patriarchs does not render the subject curse-proof, while he remains in sin. "For they are not all Israel (heirs of God with Israel) that are of Israel," that is, descended from him. "Neither, because they are the seed (natural descendants) of Abraham, are they all children," (his spiritual offspring, and heirs with him of the kingdom of God.) All are aware that the words, Israel, Israelite, Abraham's children, &c., are used in the Scriptures in two opposite senses—to designate those who have descended from these patriarchs by natural generation, and those who resemble them in moral character. Thus, Christ says to the Jews, John viii. 39: "If ye were Abraham's children (his spiritual as well as natural offspring, which you pretend to be) ye would do the works of Abraham." Again, John i. 47: "Behold an Israelite indeed, in whom is no guile!" The Jews contended that all who were the natural descendants of these patriarchs, were for that reason their spiritual offspring also. This the apostle denies in the passage just explained, and now proceeds to prove the truth of that denial.

Before attempting to elucidate or explain the passages that follow, I would invite special attention to two or three preliminary observations.

1. There were two distinct and opposite classes of persons upon whom the name of Abraham was to be called. (1.) A certain portion of those who were to descend from him through the line of Isaac. (2.) As the great founder of the sect of believers, he was to be called the father of the faithful in all subsequent ages. They were to be called his seed, and to become "heirs according to the promise."

2. Both of these alike were given to Abraham by promise—the first, in such promises as these: "At this time will I come, and Sarah shall have a son," and "In Isaac shall thy seed be called;" and the second, in the promise, "In thee and thy seed shall all the kindreds of the earth be blessed." Individuals became Abraham's seed, in the first sense, by natural birth, according to the promise in respect to Isaac. They became his offspring, in the second sense, by "walking

in the steps of the faith of our father Abraham;" that is, by embracing the faith the promise made to him. "If we are Christ's," (united to Christ by faith,) "then are we Abraham's seed, and heirs according to the promise."

3. If, now, Paul could adduce examples of natural descent from Abraham, and the other patriarchs, which did not place individuals even among their natural descendants upon whom the name of Abraham was to be called, how perfectly would he annihilate the hope of the Jew of eternal life, or of being reckoned by God among Abraham's believing offspring, and made heirs of God with him, simply because he had a place among the natural offspring of that patriarch. This, we shall see, is just what the apostle has done. "All are not Israel" (heirs with him) "who are of" (that is, the natural descendants of) "Israel." "Neither, because they are the seed" (natural offspring) "of Abraham, are they all children," induced among Abraham's spiritual descendants, and consequently heirs with him of eternal life. To sustain this proposition is the avowed object of the remaining clause of verse 7, "but, In Isaac shall thy seed be called." This declaration, which is quoted from Gen. xxi. 12. contains the affirmations not only that the name of Abraham should be called upon the descendants of Isaac, but also that it should not be called upon those of Ishmael. The descendants of the latter were not to be included among the theocratic or messianic seed of Abraham. What a strong case was this for the apostle to base his argument upon, that mere descent from Abraham did not render an individual an heir with him of eternal glory! The descendants of Ishmael, though with those of Isaac, springing from Abraham, were excluded by the Most High from being reckoned even among his messianic seed, or among his natural descendants upon whom, as such, his name was to be called. How, then, could mere descent from him place an individual with Abraham, as his spiritual ancestor, among the children of God? Moreover, the Jew himself acknowledged, in the

case of the descendants of Abraham through Ishmael, that because one is a natural descendant from that patriarch, he is not for that reason to be reckoned among Abraham's seed in either of the senses under consideration. How presumptuous, then, from his own acknowledgments, was the hope of eternal life which he had based upon the simple fact that he was one of Abraham's natural descendants!

The conclusion which the apostle deduces from the case of Isaac and Ishmael, is presented directly in verse 8. "That is, they which are the children of the flesh, (mere natural descendants from Abraham,) these are not (simply because they are thus descended) the children of God," heirs of spiritual life with Abraham: "but the children of the promise are counted for the seed." Here the principle, which I noticed above, is directly asserted; to wit, that individuals who are reckoned as Abraham's seed in either of the senses under consideration, become such, not by mere natural descent from him, but by becoming children of the promise,—the one class, by being by birth included among the natural descendants given to Abraham by the promise pertaining to Isaac, and the other, by embracing the faith, the promise pertaining to Abraham's spiritual seed.

In verse 9, the apostle simply cites the promise pertaining to Isaac, in illustration of the great truth which he had previously established.

"For this is the word of promise, At this time will I come, and Sarah shall have a son."

Such is the most triumphant argument of the apostle, based upon the example of Isaac and Ishmael. "With what amazing skill," says Mr. Morison, "and with what triumphant success the apostle has proved that there were room and verge enough for cursing to alight upon his fellow Israelites. It was true that they could boast a pure patriarchal descent; and high, certainly, was the privilege of such illustrious parentage. But the Ishmaelites were as really an Abrahamic people as they. The blood of the great 'Friend of God,' and progenitor of the Messiah, circulated in common within Ishmaelitish and Israelitish veins. Yet, the Jews themselves being judges, their cousin Ishmaelites were not a messianic people, nor elevated into the privilege of being the theocratic 'children of God.' Assuredly, then, the patriarchal ancestry of the Jews could not constitute them the people peculiar for the enjoyment of the Messiah's salvation; it could not constitute them the glory-inheriting 'sons and daughters of the Most High.' All that are 'of Israel' are not 'Israelites indeed;' neither, because they are partakers of Abraham's flesh, does it follow as a corollary, sanctioned by the logic of revelation, or the logic of reason, that they shall be partakers, as his worthy children of his honor and immortality. Everlasting life is secured by connection, not with the patriarchs, but with Christ. And if, therefore, the great mass of the apostle's 'kinsmen and brethren, according to the flesh,' disclaimed connection with that Jesus who was the only Christ, and leaned back for safety upon their connection with Abraham, Isaac, and Jacob, there can be no wonder that the apostle should mourn over the misery of their impending doom, and behold in them, with anguish, but a multiplication into millions of his former infatuated and soul-cursing self." One remark further, before leaving the cases of Isaac and Ishmael. Nothing whatever has been said by the apostle pertaining to the election or reprobation of either of these individuals or their descendants, as far *as a future state* is concerned. Nothing has yet been said that bears either directly or indirectly in favor, or upon, the doctrines of election and reprobation. The descendants of Ishmael were excluded from the messianic seed of Abraham, and thus afford perfect demonstration of the fact that even Abrahamic descent does not render one a child of God. The exclusion of Ishmael, however, neither implied that himself or posterity would or would not be finally saved, or threw the least obstacle in the way of their salvation.

The apostle now proceeds to cite a case still more in point. The Jew might object to the former argument, that Ishmael was the son of a bond-woman; though to this it might be replied, that several of the twelve tribes upon whom Abraham's name was actually called, were similarly descended. Their mothers were bond-women as well as the mother of Ishmael. Against the case of the descendants of Esau and Jacob, however, no such objection, and none of any kind, could be brought. Their ancestors were both born at the same birth, and from the same parents. Yet the descendants of Esau were, notwithstanding a patriarchal descent of the most perfect "purity" conceivable, not included in, but excluded from, the messianic seed of Abraham, the seed upon whom the name of Abraham was to be called. How, then, could the Jew hope that mere descent could place him among the spiritual seed of Abraham, and render him, even though he should reject "God's righteousness," secure against God's word of threatening? This is the precise use which, as I will now proceed to show, the apostle does make of the divine declarations and arrangements in respect to the descendants of Esau and Jacob. I will cite the entire passage pertaining to this subject, and then give the needful explanations.

"And not only *this;* but when Rebecca also had conceived by one, *even* by our father Isaac; (for *the children* being not yet born, neither having done any good or evil, that the purpose of God according to election might stand, not of works, but of him that calleth;) it was said unto her, the elder shall serve the younger. As it is written, Jacob have I loved, but Esau have I hated."

There are two verses in this passage that need a special explanation, before we consider the meaning, and bearing upon the apostle's argument of the passage entire. The first that I notice is verse 12. "It was said unto her, the elder shall serve the younger." This declaration, which is quoted from

Gen. xxv. 23, should most unquestionably be rendered thus:—The greater shall serve the less. The original word here rendered *elder*, is used forty-five times in the New Testament, and in every other instance is rendered *greater*. There is no authority for rendering it *elder*. A similar remark may be made in respect to the original word, here rendered *younger*. It is not the word that is adapted to express that idea. But who or what are we to understand as referred to, by the words *greater* and *less* in this verse? This we may learn by reference to Gen. xxv. 23, from whence it is cited. "And the Lord said unto her, two nations *are* in thy womb, and two manner of people shall be separated from thy bowels; and *the one* people shall be stronger than *the other* people; and the elder shall serve the younger." The original Hebrew word, here rendered elder, is used, as Mr. Morison observes, upwards of six hundred times in the Old Testament, and in no solitary instance can it be made to bear the meaning here given to it, with one solitary exception; and even then, as he shows, this meaning should not be given to it. Its literal meaning, as well as universal usage, requires that it should be rendered *greater*, and not *elder*. In this place, then, as well as in Romans, the phrase under consideration should be rendered:—and the *greater shall serve the less*. The meaning of the whole verse is now perfectly plain. "Two nations"—that is, the ancestors of two nations—"are in thy womb, and two manner of people shall be separated from thy bowels; and the one people shall be stronger than the other people; and the greater people shall serve the less." No reference whatever is had here to the ancestors of these peoples, nor to the relations which, as individuals, they should sustain to each other, nor to the spiritual or eternal destiny of either, or of that of their posterity. But it is said that one of these people should become stronger than the other, and that the greater should finally be subjected to the less,—facts which actually occurred in the subsequent history of these nations. In saying, however, that these people should constitute two nations, instead of being blended into, and thus together constituting the messianic seed of Abraham, as the descendants of the twelve patriarchs did, it is affirmed that one of them should constitute the messianic seed of Abraham, while the other people should be excluded from that relation. Nor was there anything in this divine revelation to Rebecca, intimating directly or indirectly, clearly or obscurely, which of these people should be the greater or which the less, or which should constitute the messianic seed, or which should be excluded from it. Of this fact both Isaac and Rebecca remained profoundly ignorant, till after Jacob obtained and Esau lost the blessing. The communication did imply, however, as I have said, that the one people should constitute the messianic seed, and the other be excluded from it, and thus laid the foundation for the unanswerable argument of the apostle; that, inasmuch as the purest conceivable patriarchal descent was not of itself sufficient to place the subject even among the messianic people upon whom the name of Abraham was to be called, much less could it of itself, as the Jew contended, place that subject among the children of God, as the spiritual seed of Abraham.

The verse following the one now under consideration next deserves attention. As it is written, "Jacob have I loved, but Esau have I hated." By referring to Mal. i. 2, 3, from which this verse is taken, you will perceive clearly, that the terms, *Jacob* and *Esau*, as here used, refer not at all to them as individuals, but exclusively to their posterity. "I loved Jacob, (the descendants of Jacob,) and I hated Esau, (the descendants of Esau,) and laid his mountains and his heritage waste." Among the Hebrews, when one object is loved less than another, and when one is treated with less severity than another, the one is said to be loved and the other hated. Thus, in Gen. xxix. 33, Leah says that she was "hated" of her husband, while the same idea is presented in the verse preceding, in which it is said "that Jacob loved Rachael more than Leah." The meaning of these words in the passage before us is, that God had brought the most desolating judgments upon the descendants of Esau, while he had spared those of Jacob. The love here referred to was not the love of an eternal election, nor the hatred that of eternal and unconditional reprobation, of Jacob or Esau, or of the posterity of either. They refer simply and exclusively to temporal mercies and judgments bestowed and inflicted with a wise and righteous discrimination.

But, in verse 11, we read of an "election," and of "a purpose of God according to (in respect to) election." We now learn distinctly and undeniably to what that purpose and election referred. 1. They refer not at all to the individuals as such, to wit, Jacob and Esau, but exclusively to their posterity. 2. They simply refer to one as the elected messianic seed of Abraham, and exclude the other from that seed. 3. They have no reference whatever to the spiritual and eternal destiny of either people, but simply to the temporal relations which one should sustain to the other. *The greater people shall serve the less.* 4. No argument whatever can be adduced from this passage in favor of, or, in the least, bearing upon, the *doctrine* of eternal and unconditional election and reprobation. No reference whatever can be shown in the passage, anywhere, to either of these doctrines. But why does the apostle I say, "For the children being not yet born, neither having done any good or evil," &c.? The reason is obvious. The Jew might reply to the apostle's argument, based upon the example of Esau and Jacob, on this wise. To be sure the posterity of Esau was excluded from, and those of Jacob included in, the messianic seed of Abraham. The reasons for this distinction, however, are found in the overshadowing merit of Jacob. To exclude such a resort, he is reminded that the communication under consideration was made before either was born, or had done any good or evil,—that is, had any moral character whatever that could constitute the basis of the election between them. The election and purpose in respect to these peoples, constituting one the messianic seed of Abraham, and excluding the other from it, were an election and purpose "not of works," that is, they had not their basis in the merits or demerits of the ancestors of these peoples, and thus affording ground of boasting to the Jew. They were of "Him that calleth," that is, had their basis in the good pleasure of God.

The bearings of this case of Jacob and Esau upon the apostle's argument, against the position of the Jew, that descent from the patriarchs, of itself, secured him a place among the children of God, and consequently rendered him secure against God's word of threatening, even though he should reject the offer of mercy through Christ, is perfectly obvious. 1. Their posterity stood in a perfect equality, as far as patriarchal descent is concerned. 2. Before any merit or demerit attached to either Jacob or Esau, and consequently before any ground of preference on the part of the posterity of either, consequent on superior ancestral merit, did or could exist, the purpose of God to elect the posterity of one as constituting the messianic seed, and the rejection of the other from that relation, was announced by God. 3. As a place even among the messianic seed was not at all conditioned on mere patriarchal merit or descent, but upon the good pleasure of God, how could the Jew hope that through such descent and merit, and that only, he could have a place among the spiritual seed of Abraham? 4. In the case of the descendants of Esau, the Jew himself acknowledged that there was the purest conceivable patriarchal descent, with an actual exclusion from a place among the messianic seed, and with no title on that account to a place among the children of God, and no security consequently against God's word of threatening, in case of a rejection of "God's righteousness." Why, then, should the Jew rest his hope of eternal life upon a foundation which he himself acknowledged had proved wholly inadequate in the case of others?

REMARKS.

We have thus traversed the important portion of the Bible which attention was to be directed in this lecture. What have we found in it? 1. We have found clearly and undeniably set forth one of the great cardinal doctrines of Christianity—the divinity and humanity of our Lord and Saviour.

2. We have found also this great truth set forth and implied in the reasoning of he apostle; that if we neglect the great salvation presented to our faith through Christ, nothing can shield us from the curse of God.

3. We have also learned another important truth, that the highest privileges, the clearest light, and the choicest influences of Heaven, may consist with utter and final reprobation, and, if unimproved, will combine their influence to render our doom infinitely the more aggravated.

4. We have seen the entire passage to possess a beautiful consistency throughout; all the propositions, arguments, illustrations, and facts, adduced by the sacred writer, culminating in one grand conclusion, and sweeping away with resistless force the refuge of lies, where the Jew had concealed himself, in the vain hope that he was thereby secure against God's word of threatening.

5. In our sojourn amid the great realities shadowed forth to our apprehension in this passage, we have searched in vain for a place for that great stumbling-block in the way of the salvation of sinners, the doctrines of eternal and unconditional election and reprobation. In traversing through the length and breadth of the apostle's reasonings, we have found not a solitary nook or corner where these dogmas have a legitimate dwelling-place.

LECTURE II.

Verses 14—18.

RECAPITULATION OF THE POSITION ELUCIDATED IN THE FIRST LECTURE.

In the first five verses of this chapter, Paul, as we have seen, affirms, in the most solemn manner, his great heaviness and sorrow of heart, on account of the impending doom of the mass of his brethren and kindred, the Jews.

He also states certain circumstances connected with the Jews which made their then state, and consequent prospective doom, sources of such anguish to his mind. 1. He had himself once been in the same state of mind in which they then were, and exposed to the same doom that was impending over them. They were wishing themselves accursed from Christ. He had once willed the same thing relatively to himself. 2. They were the descendants of the holy patriarchs and the greatest honors and privileges attached to them, consequent on their relations as the messianic seed of such patriarchs.

In referring to the relations and privileges of his countrymen consequent on their patriarchal descent, Paul presents, in the strongest possible light, the very facts on which the Jew rested his hope of eternal life, and denied his exposure to any threatenings which God has denounced against sinners. Paul admits the facts, and admits them in all their length and breadth; but denies the conclusion which the Jew based upon them.

To sustain and demonstrate the truth of that denial is the object of the apostle, in all his reasonings from verse 6, and onwards through the chapter. He admits the patriarchal descent of the Jew, and the high honors and privileges pertaining to him as the messianic seed of Abraham. But the case of the Jew, in consequence of these facts, is not, he says, such that God's word of threatening has lost its curse-inflicting power in reference to him, because he is a Jew, any more than it has in reference to other sinners; and that for this reason all the natural descendants of Israel are not his spiritual offspring; nor, because men are the mere lineal descendants of Abraham, are they all his spiritual children. If this was so, as the Jew claimed that it was, then, whatever threatenings God may have denounced against sinners, such denunciations could have no efficacy as far as the Jew was concerned. He was curse-proof, consequent on his relations to Abraham. You are not curse-proof, is the argument of the apostle, for the all-sufficient reason, that all the lineally descended offspring of the patriarchs are not, as a matter of fact—a fact which you yourself acknowledge—their spiritual offspring, and, consequently, heirs with them of eternal life. To demonstrate the truth of this denial of the position of the Jew, is the object of the apostle in citing the cases of the descendants of Abraham, through Ishmael and Esau.

In reference to both these people, the Jew himself admitted the following conclusions, which were of the most vital bearing upon the apostle's position. 1. Their descent was really and truly patriarchal, and that of the posterity of Esau of the purest possible kind. 2. Yet such descent did not secure for them a place even among the messianic seed of Abraham. How, then, could such descent merely place the Jew among Abraham's spiritual offspring, and render him curse-proof against God's word of threatening? 3. That this descent did not, in fact, do this in reference to the posterity of Ishmael and Esau, the Jew himself confessed and affirmed. How presumptuous in him, then, to suppose that such descent could shield him from God's word of threatening, if he should reject God's righteousness!

To cut the Jew off from all hope resting on mere patriarchal descent, the apostle reminds him that God's purpose to elect one part of the descendants of Isaac as the messianic seed of Abraham, and to exclude the other, was announced when the ancestors of these peoples had neither merit nor demerit that could constitute them heirs of such election. Those ancestors were not yet born, and neither of them had done anything good or evil. If God made a discrimination among even the descendants of Isaac, in making up the messianic seed of Abraham, what reason had the Jew to conclude that a discrimination, if reasons, such as a rejection of God's righteousness, should demand it, would not be made among the posterity of Israel, in making up the spiritual offspring of Abraham?

That I have rightly explained the object of the apostle in his reasonings against the error of the Jew, and in the use which he makes of the cases of the descendants of Ishmael and Esau, I presume no one will doubt. How clearly is this shown in the conclusion which the apostle draws from the case of the descendants of Isaac and Ishmael, in verses 7 and 8, "In Isaac shall thy seed be called;" that is, your name shall be called upon your posterity descending through Isaac, and not upon those through Ishmael. Now mark the conclusion which the apostle deduces from this declaration: "that is," in other words, this example proves at "they which are children of the flesh, (mere lineal descendants of the patriarchs,) these are not (merely for that reason) the children of God." The Jew said they were, and were consequently, whatever they might do, shielded from God's word of threatening. The conclusion which Paul draws from the example of Isaac and Ishmael, shows that his object in adducing their case was to disprove the affirmation. For the express and avowed object of sustaining the same position, he proceeds to cite the case of Jacob and Esau. I have not, then, misapprehended the great object or design of the apostle in the portion of the chapter which we have already considered. This, I presume, all will admit. If this be admitted, two conclusions necessarily follow from that admission. 1. I have also rightly interpreted the particular passages of which the whole is made up; for I have so interpreted them, and only so, as to render their real meaning harmonious with the great design under consideration. No opposite or different explanations can be made to fall in with that design. 2. No place whatever is found, in the first thirteen verses of this chapter, for the doctrines of eternal and unconditional election and reprobation. Nothing that we have yet found even looks towards these doctrines.

Explanation of Romans ix., *verses* 14—18.

We now advance to a direct consideration of the passage which I shall attempt to explain and elucidate in this lecture. In respect to the design of the apostle, in this passage, there can be no doubt. It is to answer an objection which a Jew would naturally urge against his position and argument in the preceding part of the chapter, and to answer it in such a way as to confirm and strengthen that position and argument. Permit me to ask a question or two here. Would the introduction of the doctrines of eternal and unconditional election and reprobation tend to any such result? What appropriate place could they have in such a connection as this? What tendency has such a doctrine to prove that God is not unjust in not making mere patriarchal descent the condition of eternal life? Can anybody in the wide world tell us how?

But to the passage itself, "What shall we say then?" that is, what conclusion shall we deduce from the doctrine which has been demonstrated as true in the preceding part of the chapter, to wit, that the Jew, merely because he is a lineal descendant of Abraham and the patriarchs, is not, for that reason merely, an heir of glory with Abraham, and curse-proof in respect to God's word of threatening denounced against all who reject God's righteousness, which is through faith in Christ? "Is there unrighteousness with God?" that is, is this the conclusion we shall draw from such a fact? Shall we conclude that if God does not save the Jew, however wicked, and doom to eternal death the Gentile, however holy,—and that simply because the one is and the other is not a descendant of Abraham and the other patriarchs, that therefore God is not righteous in his dispensations? "God forbid;" that is, it is not so by any means.

To show this, the apostle makes a direct appeal to what was recorded in the Scriptures, as having been said by God to Moses. The Jew acknowledged the divine authority of what was there written. If, then, Paul could show, that his doctrine was clearly and undeniably taught in the Jewish Scriptures themselves, the objection of the Jew against it would be perfectly silenced. This is the very appeal to which he now resorts: "For he saith to Moses, I will have mercy on whom I will have mercy, and I will have compassion on whom I will have compassion." The term "For," in the commencement of this verse, shows what Paul's object is in citing the words of God to Moses. There is not unrighteousness with God in dealing with the Jew according to the principle which I have laid down and established. "For he (God) saith unto Moses:" that is, the very doctrine which I maintain is affirmed in the declaration of God to Moses, which I will now cite. If this declaration, then, is rightly explained, it will be so explained as to affirm that doctrine. To show that it does contain this doctrine, let us now recur to the circumstances in which this declaration of God to Moses was made. The declaration is cited from Ex. xxxiii. 19. It was also made directly and immediately with reference to the Jews. Whatever principle of the divine administration, therefore, is contained in it, the Jew himself would acknowledge was applicable to him. What, then, were the circumstances in which this declaration was made? Moses had been for forty days and forty nights in the mount with God. During this time God had written the Ten Commandments with his own finger on the two tablets of stone. While this solemn scene was being enacted in the mount, the people in the camp had made a golden calf, and were around it engaged in the most obscene and idolatrous worship. God reminded Moses of the fearful fact, and proposed to him to destroy the whole people, and make of him a great nation. Moses entreated God not to do this, but to spare the people. He then went down among the people, destroyed their idol, inflicted due vengeance upon the heading idolaters, and then reascended the mount and besought the Lord to pardon the sin of the people. This petition and God's answer are found in Ex. xxxii. 32—34. "Yet now, if thou wilt forgive their sin—; and if not, blot me, I pray thee, out of thy book which thou hast written. And the lord said unto Moses, Whosoever hath sinned against me, him will I blot out of my book. Therefore, now go, lead the people unto *the place* of which I have spoken unto thee to behold, mine angel shall go before thee, nevertheless in the day when I visit I will visit their sin upon them." Here you will observe that God answered the prayer of Moses so far as sparing the lives of the people was concerned. He peremptorily denied his request, however, as far as the petition for the *pardon* of their sin was concerned. He proposed to spare the people's lives, to permit an angel of his to go before them and head them into the promised land; but threatened to take his own presence from their midst, and not to head them in as his people. Moses afterwards appeared before God to get this fearful threatening of the withdrawment of the Shekinah removed. God heard him even here. "My presence (face) shall go with thee." Then Moses presented one petition in his own behalf. "I beseech Thee, show me thy glory." To this petition God also acceded. In doing so, however, he reminded Moses of the petition which he had presented for the *pardon* of the people. As far as this is concerned, is the divine response, my principles of administration are fixed and changeless. If you ask me to forgive those who are sinning against me, I cannot grant the request. I receive no dictation from creatures in respect to the conditions on which I shall pardon the sinner. On the other hand, "I will have mercy on whom I will have mercy, and I will have compassion on whom I will have compassion;" that is, I have my own conditions on which I will pardon sin, and the petitions of no individuals, in behalf of those, whoever they may be, who have not complied with these conditions, can avail with me. This is the plain meaning of this remarkable declaration of God to Moses. Mark, now, its bearing upon the apostle's argument with the Jew. The Jew affirmed that although he should sin, and continue in it, he was shielded from the threatened curse, by his relations to Abraham. Paul adduces a case in which even Moses prayed for the removal of the curse which hung over Jews themselves, who were yet in their sins; and God positively refused to grant his request, and left the curse still suspended, without mitigation, over the transgressor. No, says God. I cannot grant such a request. "I will have mercy on whom I will have mercy," &c. How, then, could the Jew hope, while remaining in the same state, that the merits of Abraham would shield him from the curse which God still suspended over him? Such is the argument of the apostle in adducing this saying of God to Moses.

Observe, now, the conclusion which the apostle bases upon this declaration of God to Moses: "So, then, it is not of him that willeth, nor of him that runneth, but of God that showeth mercy;" that is, it follows from the declaration of God to Moses just cited. What is it that follows from this declaration? This: that the *condition* of mercy does not depend upon the will of him that seeks mercy, nor upon that of him who runs after it, but upon the will of God who shows or exercises mercy. If it belongs to God to dispense mercy, it belongs to him also to prescribe the condition on which he will dispense it. The Jew was seeking mercy and running after it; but, instead of inquiring after the condition on which God had promised to bestow it, he was prescribing conditions for God. He consequently remained ignorant of "God's righteousness" or method of salvation, and, in "going about to establish his own righteousness," refused to "submit to the righteousness of God." God had said to Moses, "I will have mercy," &c. It became the Jew, then, not to say God must save this man and destroy that; but to inquire who it is that God will bestow mercy upon; and, by becoming such, to receive that mercy himself.

The mistake of the high Calvinist, in his explanation of this passage, is this: he does not inquire what it is that "is not of him that willeth," &c., but concludes that the word "it" refers to conversion or election, instead of pardon. To suppose that this term refers to Conversion, or eternal and unconditional election, and not to the *condition* of pardon, is a violation of all the laws of interpretation. Nothing whatever has been said in the chapter about conversion or election, or any such doctrine, one way or the other. The *condition* of mercy on the other hand, is the point, and the only point at issue, in this connection, between the apostle and the Jew. The term "it," then, according to all the laws of language, must represent this idea. How important it was for the Jew to understand this great truth. He was earnestly seeking for mercy, and was running his round of ceremonies to obtain it, but was prescribing conditions of his own, instead of inquiring after God's way of life, and thus "submitting to God's righteousness." The truth, then, that he needed to be reminded of, is the fact that the *condition* of mercy does not depend upon the will of him that seeks it, nor upon that of him that runs after it, but upon the will of God who bestows it. This is the sentiment, and the only sentiment, expressed by the apostle in this passage.

In further confirmation of the truth thus clearly established, Paul next adduces the case of Pharaoh. "For the Scripture saith unto Pharaoh, Even for this same purpose have I raised thee up, that I might show my power in thee, and that my name might be declared throughout all the earth." The term "for" connects this verse with what goes before, and shows that the object of the apostle, in adducing this case, is to elucidate and confirm the doctrine which he has just set forth. There must be something in this saying to Pharaoh, therefore, which bears directly and decisively upon that doctrine. The doctrine is this, that God will have mercy upon those who comply with his own divinely prescribed condition, and upon none others, whatever their relations or circumstances may be. What, then, is there in this inspired declaration to Pharaoh that elucidates and confirms this great truth? Let us see if we can find in it this important principle. The first clause of the declaration is this: "For this cause have I raised thee up." The Greek word here rendered "raised up" is applied when an individual is raised from any condition in which he was before, to a higher or different state. For example: If he is asleep, to raise up, means to awaken out of sleep; if he is dead, to raise from death to life; and if he is sick, to restore to health. The literal meaning of the original Hebrew word which the Greek term under consideration represents, in the connection in which it is found, (Ex. ix. 16,) means, to cause to stand. They indicate that Pharaoh had been raised up from some state in which he had been before these words were addressed to him. What was that state? Pharaoh and all his people had just been restored from the fearful plague of the "boils breaking out with blains upon man and upon beast." God appears before him, through his servants Moses and Aaron, and tells him that if he will continue to rebel against his word, he will go on with his judgments for the purpose of convincing Pharaoh and his people that there was "none like God in all the earth." "For I will at this time send all my plagues upon thine heart, and upon thy servants, and upon thy people, that thou mayest know that there is none like me in all the earth. For now I will stretch out my hand, that I may smite thee and thy people with pestilence, and thou shalt be cut off from the earth." In such a connection, and just as Pharaoh had been restored from such a disease, the words before us were addressed to him. "And in very deed for this cause have I raised thee up." Raising from the bed of sickness, and restoration from the fearful disease which had just fallen upon him, was the raising up referred to. Calling into being, cannot be the meaning of these words in this connection. The words rendered raised up, never, I believe, have this signification. The idea of raising up to the throne of Egypt, is also too remote from the circumstances in which the words were uttered to be the raising up referred to.

But for what purpose was Pharaoh raised up? Two reasons are assigned, "that I might show my power in thee"—"and that my name might be declared throughout all the earth." What is the meaning of the first clause? Paul speaks of God's having "revealed his Son in him." The meaning in this case cannot be mistaken. It means not only that God made Christ known to Paul, but that a union was consummated between Paul and Christ, by means of that revelation. To reveal God's power in an individual, then, implies, that the individual has not only received the knowledge of God, but has come into harmony with the truth revealed to him. The first object of God, therefore, in restoring Pharaoh to health, and preserving him as he had done, was to secure, by means of that revelation, his salvation. The salvation of Pharaoh, then, was God's first object in all his dealings with him.

But what was the second? "And that my name might be declared throughout all the earth;" that is, through you, as a monument of grace, should you repent, or a monument of wrath, should my judgments fail of their primary object in respect to you, to bring about a consummation in which, for the salvation of the race, "God's name should be declared throughout all the earth." Such is the evident meaning of this very extensively misunderstood, and, consequently, fearfully perverted, passage. Instead of calling this unfortunate man into being, or raising him to the throne of Egypt, for the purpose of making him, for the terror of mankind, a monument of wrath, God is here revealed as sparing the guilty man, in the midst of the most terrific judgments, and restoring him from a deadly disease, with none other than purposes of mercy to him and to the race, with no intent of resorting to reprobating judgment, till all efforts to prevent such a doom had become perfectly hopeless.

To render the truth of this explanation still more evident, permit me to recur again to the connection in which this passage stands in Ex. ix. According to the celebrated Hebrew grammarian, Dr. Isaac Nordheimer, and many other learned biblical scholars, the preceding verse should be thus rendered: "For should I now stretch out my hand, and smite thee and thy people with pestilence, thou wouldst be cut off from the earth;" that is, should I bring down my judgments as I might do, you would be cut off from the earth, and thereby your probation being brought to a sudden and final termination, you would have no other opportunity to obtain mercy. In the 14th verse, God informs Pharaoh that for the purpose of securing his salvation and that of his people, by convincing them that there was "none like him (God) in all the earth," he would, "at that time, send all his plagues upon him, and upon his servants, and upon his people." In the next verse, the one above explained, to show the monarch how completely he was in God's hands, God reminds him that if he should, as he might do, "stretch out his hand and smite Pharaoh and his people with pestilence, (with destructive disease, instead of plagues, under which life might be preserved,) he would be cut off from the earth;" his probation thereby being at once terminated, and no further opportunity afforded him "for repentance unto life." Then, in the next verse, that cited by Paul, God adds, "And in very deed, for this cause," that is, to prevent thy destruction, by lengthening out thy probation, on the one hand, and by "showing thee my power" to secure thy salvation, on the other, "I have raised thee up," (restored thee to health, and preserved thee alive in the midst of my judgments.) This, God informed Pharaoh, was his direct and immediate design, as far as he as an individual was concerned. But he had another ulterior design. Through Pharaoh, as a monument of mercy—should he repent, or of judgment—should God's dispensations fail of their end, in respect to him is an individual, he designed, for the salvation of the race, to bring about a consummation in which "His (God's) name should be declared (revealed or made known) throughout all the earth." As a vessel of mercy or of wrath, Pharaoh was to be, in the hands of God, an instrument of good to the race. The latter God would not render him till all hope of his repentance was annihilated, by his incorrigible resistance to God's efforts for his salvation. Such, I repeat, is the real meaning of this very commonly misunderstood and fearfully perverted passage. When rightly expounded, it wears but one aspect, that of infinite benignity blended with beneficent but awful judgment, the only aspect becoming the face of God.

But how does this example bear upon the apostle's argument? The Jew maintained that no individual, a descendant of Abraham and within the pale of the Jewish community, could be lost. He was shielded against the curse of God, and secure of pardon, whatever his sins might be, in consequence of his relations to the patriarchs. It would imply unrighteousness in God, were a Jew lost, and a Gentile saved, whatever the character of either might be. To convince his countrymen, and that from their own Scriptures, that they were wholly and most fatally deceived, in holding such dogmas, Paul adduces the sayings of God to Moses on the one hand, and to Pharaoh on the other. In these passages the following great facts, bearing directly and most decisively upon the question at issue, stand most distinctly and undeniably revealed. 1. When expressly entreated, even by Moses, to pardon Jews, while in their sins, God refused to grant the request. How could the Jew, then, without repentance, expect to escape the judgment of God? 2. God pledged himself, even to Pharaoh, that he should be forgiven, if he would repent; and finally brought reprobating judgments upon that guilty man, only when all further efforts for his salvation were hopeless. The Jewish dogma, then, was in palpable opposition to God's own revealed principles of administration in respect to Jews and Gentiles both. The sentiments of Paul, on the other hand, involved no "unrighteousness in God," no forfeiture of his word, because they accorded perfectly with the express revelation of God, in the Jewish Scriptures themselves. 3. The Jew was, at that very time, in circumstances precisely similar to that in which Pharaoh was when God's message of mercy and judgment was conveyed to him, and should be admonished, by the final doom of that monarch, not to incur similar judgments, by hardening himself against God, as that man had done. Thus we see that the sayings of God to Moses, on the one hand, and to Pharaoh, on the other, were of most vital bearing upon the question at issue between Paul and his brethren the Jews. They were perfectly decisive of the whole argument.

We now advance to a consideration of verse 18, into which all the previous reasonings of the apostle culminate. "Therefore hath he mercy on whom he will *have mercy,* and whom he will he hardeneth." The word "therefore" shows the connection of this verse with what goes before. The true sense of the verse obviously depends upon the meaning to be attached to the words "hath mercy" and "hardeneth." Of the meaning of the former words there can be no doubt. Mercy and pardon are synonymous terms, and are used in the same sense throughout the Scriptures, when applied to the same subject. The literal meaning of the term harden is, to render an object hard. When applied to moral agents it means, primarily, to render obstinate, reprobate; and, secondly, to render to such, as have rendered themselves reprobate, deserved retributions, in which case it stands opposed to, or is the opposite of, mercy. In this last sense it is obviously to be understood in the passage before us. As the meaning of the words "hath mercy" is known to be to bestow pardon, the meaning of the opposite term, "harden," must be, to render to those who render themselves incorrigible, deserved retributions. The meaning of the whole verse may be thus expressed. God, as is evident from what has been shown from the divine declarations to Moses and Pharaoh, has, in opposition to the Jewish idea, that in the exercise of mercy he is confined to the Jew, and of judgment to the Gentile, his own principles of administration, in conformity to which he pardons whom he will, and punishes whom he will. The idea is not that God renders holy whom he will, and sinful whom he will, or that he eternally elects or reprobates whom he will. The apostle has no reference either direct or indirect to any such dogmas. He is speaking exclusively in opposition to the Jewish error which confined the exercise of mercy and judgment to natural descent and outward condition, instead of its being dispensed according to character, without reference to any other circumstances. God, the apostle would assure us, is not, in his dispensations, bound down by any humanly prescribed conditions. He has his own principles according to which mercy and judgment are dispensed, and, if we would obtain the one and avoid the other, we must not go about to establish a righteousness of our own; but learn of God what his principles of administration are, and, by submitting to his righteousness, become partakers of the "great salvation."

The mistake of the high Calvinist, in his explanation of this passage, lies here. He assumes that the words "hath mercy" refer to conversion; whereas they never bear this meaning. While he assumes this, in opposition to all the laws of correct interpretation, he shrinks from the conclusion to which such a construction necessarily conducts us, to wit, that the opposite word, "hardeneth," must, in that case, mean to render sinful and confirm in sin. If the words "hath mercy" do refer to conversion, the term "hardeneth" must mean to render incorrigible in sin, which it would be impious in us to impute to God. No explanation of any passage which does, of necessity, impute such a principle to God, can be correct, or should be admitted as such.

REMARKS.

1. In the Scriptures, God is, in some few instances, as in the case of Pharaoh, said to harden the hearts of individuals. What meaning should we attach to such declarations? In reply, I would remark that God is said, in the Scriptures, to bring an event to pass,—1. When he is the efficient cause of such event. 2. When he does that from which the event necessarily results. 3. When he does that which is the mere occasion, but in no sense the efficient cause, of the event. Thus, Christ, by his coming into the world, sent fire on the earth. In this last sense, exclusively, God hardens the hearts of creatures. He simply, in the accomplishment of his own benevolent purposes, does that, in resisting which, they harden their own hearts.

2. We now see how totally the apostle's reasonings and purposes, throughout this whole chapter, must be perverted to draw from it any such doctrines as that of eternal and unconditional election and reprobation. His fundamental aim must be wholly overlooked, and his entire course of argument turned from its true end, to make him teach any such doctrines.

3. What a divine aspect the dealings of God with Pharaoh wear, when rightly expounded, as contrasted with that which the high Calvinistic explanation puts upon the case! Mercy and judgment cannot be blended so as to wear a sweeter majesty and more awful love than in this example, when rightly understood. Yet high predestinarian explanation has imparted a spirit of gloom and terror to it, which has long thrown the glory, and love, and justice of God into a deep and dark eclipse.

LECTURE III.

Verses 19—24.
RECAPITULATION.

A FEW words may be requisite in developing the exposition given in the last lecture, of the 14th—18th verses of this chapter, before proceeding to the explanation of the passage which is to occupy our attention on the present occasion. The apostle, having most fully demonstrated, by an induction of undeniable facts—facts bearing directly and decisively upon the subject—that the Jew could not be secure of God's favor, and curse-proof in respect to God's word of threatening against those who reject his righteousness, simply on the ground of patriarchal descent, asks the question, v. 14, "What shall we say unto these things?" that is, what conclusion shall we draw from them? Shall we conclude that if God does not save the Jew, however wicked, and reprobate to eternal death the Gentile, however holy, that God is unrighteous in his dispensations! "God forbid!"

That God is not unrighteous in his dispensations holding his word of threatening over the Jew as was over the Gentile, while he continues to reject God's righteousness, and to save all alike, whether Jew or Gentile, who accept that righteousness, the apostle now makes a direct appeal to the writings of Moses, whose authority the Jew himself acknowledged as divine. God is not unrighteous, is the argument of the apostle, in treating men according to the principle which I have laid down. This is evident from his declaration to Moses. God, in answer to the prayer of Moses, had averted his threatening of destroying the people from the earth, and, while he spared them, to take his presence from them. But when Moses prayed that God would *pardon* the people, they being yet in their sins, and expressed a willingness, as a means of securing this blessing to the people, that God should blot him out of his book, God refused to answer his request. He would neither forgive the sinner remaining in his sins, nor would he blot out of his book those who had repented. On the other hand, his principles of administration were fixed and changeless. "He would have mercy on whom he would have mercy, and have compassion on whom he would have compassion." The prayer of no individual, or any other considerations, could avail to induce any change in the divine administration, in this respect. This declaration of God to Moses, the apostle proceeds to show, v. 16, clearly establishes one great principle of God's administration, to wit, that the *condition* on which God will dispense mercy to man does not depend upon the will of him who seeks it, nor upon the will of him who uses means to obtain it, but upon the will of God who bestows it. If it belongs to God to exercise mercy, it belongs to him to say upon what condition he will dispense it. The creature, then, instead of prescribing for God the condition of mercy, should humbly inquire of God what his condition is, and, by compliance with that condition, enjoy it himself. "So, then," that is, it follows from the declaration of God to Moses, just cited, that "it," the condition on which pardon is bestowed by God, "is not of him that willeth (seeks) nor of him that runneth;" that is, it is not for men, in seeking mercy and using means to obtain it, to say on what condition they shall receive it, "but of God that showeth mercy;" that is, it is for God, who is to show mercy, to say on what condition he will confer it. The Jew was prescribing for God. Paul informs him that God himself has revealed the fact that it belongs to God to prescribe conditions to him. If, therefore, he would not fail of heaven, he must humbly learn of God what the condition of life prescribed by him is, and by compliance render his salvation sure.

The same great truth, the apostle goes on to say, is confirmed still further by the divine declaration to Pharaoh. God had afflicted that self-hardened sinner with successive judgments of the most awful kind. He had especially just raised him up from, a disease of the most fearful character—that of "boils breaking out with blains upon man and upon beast." God now sends his divinely-inspired servants, Moses and Aaron, to him, to inform him, that to convince him and his servants that "there was none like him in all the earth," he would still go on bringing one plague upon them after an other, adding that "if he should go on, as he might do, and smite him and his people with pestilence, they would be cut off from the earth," and thereby their probation cease, and their salvation become impossible. God had, however, acted upon a different principle. For the sake of saving him from the doom that was impending over him, and doing it by showing him his power, he "had raised him up" from the fearful disease from which he had just been restored. That was God's first design in regard to him. He had also an ulterior purpose. By him, as a monument of grace, should he repent, or a monument of wrath, should he refuse to repent, God designed to bring about a consummation in which "His name should be declared throughout all the earth," that by means of that revelation, men might everywhere be brought to a saving knowledge of the truth. "For this cause," to give you additional opportunities, and bring additional influences upon you to secure your salvation, "I have raised thee up," restored thee from thy recent sickness, "that I might show my power in thee," (show thee my power according to the Hebrew;) that is, by a revelation of myself to thee, and in thee, to secure thy salvation, and succeeding or failing in this, and treating you accordingly, as a monument of grace or wrath, to bring about such a result; that is, my name shall be "declared throughout all the earth."

From these two sayings of God, the one to Moses and the other to Pharaoh, in the first of which God refused to forgive the impenitent Jew, though even Moses prayed for his forgiveness; and in the second, God promised to forgive even Pharaoh, if he would repent, how evident is the apostle's conclusion, that God has his own changeless principles, on which he will dispense mercy on the one hand, and punish the incorrigible on the other; and that, in selecting his vessels of mercy and vessels of wrath according to these principles, he is not, as the Jew supposed, confined to any people or nation. "Therefore," that is, it undeniably results from all that I have said, "hath he mercy on whom he will have mercy, and whom he will he hardeneth;" that is, God is gracious towards, or pardons, whom he will, and is hard towards reprobates, or inflicts the penalty of the law upon whom he will. The object of the apostle here is, and this is the principle, and only principle, in which his whole previous argument culminates;—his object, I say, is to affirm that God,—in opposition to the idea of the Jew, that God, in the exercise of mercy, was confined to the Jews, and in the exercise of judgment to the Gentiles,—had his own fixed and unalterable principles of administration, and that, in conformity to those principles, he selected his vessels of honor and dishonor, without respect to the will of man, or his mere relations as a Jew or a Gentile. Paul affirms, and designs to affirm, no such principle as this, that God makes holy whom he will, and makes sinful whom he will. The apostle is not speaking at all of God's agency in the production of moral character in man, but exclusively of the principles of his administration in dispensing mercy or judgment in view of character already formed. The position of the Jew was, that mercy and wrath should both alike be dispensed with exclusive reference to external condition, and not at all with reference to character. Paul maintains, on the contrary, that they are bestowed exclusively, not with reference to mere national descent at all, but according to character, as sinful or holy. The sovereignty for which the Jew contended was one which confined God's electing grace to the Jew, and His reprobating wrath to the Gentile. The sovereignty for which Paul contended, was God's high prerogative to select his vessels of honor and dishonor, according to his own revealed, fixed, and changeless principle of treating men in conformity to moral character, and to select them from the Jews and Gentiles indiscriminately. To deny, as the result of his previous demonstrations, the Jewish principle of partialism, and affirm God's principle of universal and impartial love and justice, is Paul's exclusive object, when he says, "Therefore hath he mercy on whom he will *have mercy,* and whom he will he hardeneth."

Explanation of Romans ix. 19—24.

"Thou wilt say them unto me, why doth he yet find fault? for who hath resisted his will? Nay, but, oh man, who art thou that repliest against God? Shall the thing formed say to him that formed *it,* Why hast thou made me thus? Hath not the potter power, over the clay, of the same lump to make one vessel unto honor and another unto dishonor? *What* if God, willing to show *his* wrath, and to make his power known, endured with much long-suffering the vessels of wrath fitted to destruction; and that he might make known the riches of his glory on the vessels of mercy which he had afore prepared unto glory, even us whom he hath called, not of the Jews only, but also of the Gentiles?"

Verse 19 requires very special consideration, as it is the stronghold in which the advocate of unconditional predestination entrenches himself. His explanation of the passage is this:—Paul having established the doctrine, that all events, the actions of men, and consequently their character and eternal destiny among the rest, are rendered fixed, certain, and unalterable by an eternal and all-necessitating decree, the Jew comes forward with this objection against the doctrine, to wit, that as God's will determines the actions of men irresistibly, and as no man consequently can resist it, God, therefore, has no right to blame men for what they do. This is supposed to be the objection of the Jew to the doctrine of election and reprobation which Paul had presented. In reply, I would direct special attention to the following considerations:—

1. Let us suppose that Paul had really taught this doctrine, to wit, that God, by an eternal all-necessitating decree, has rendered it impossible for those who sin to be holy in the circumstances in which he has placed them, and then dooms them to eternal death, for doing what he himself has rendered it impossible for them not to do. Let us then suppose the Jew had seriously asked the question, on what grounds can God blame me for doing what himself has rendered it impossible for me not to do? What answer, satisfactory to a reasonable mind, could be given to such a question? There are some things which the Bible itself teaches us it would not be right in God to do; as, for example, to forgive the sinner without an atonement. So we are taught, Rom. iii. 26, "That God has set forth Christ to be a propitiation through faith in his blood, that God might be just, and the justifier of him that believeth in Jesus;" clearly implying that it would be unjust in God to forgive sin without the atonement. Now, if it would be unjust in God to forgive sin, but for the sacrifice of Christ, how could it be just in him to punish creatures eternally for doing, what he himself, in the fulfilment of an eternal decree, has rendered it impossible for them not to do? You may, if you please, *say* that it would be right, and charge the objector with replying against God. But can you tell us, or can you yourself see, *how* it can be right? You may say that God has the power to do it; he has power, as far as mere ability is concerned, to forgive the sinner without an atonement. To have the power, and to possess the right, to do a certain act, are quite different things. Can you yourself, hearer, see how it would be right in God to send creatures to hell eternally for not performing what is to them, and what has been rendered to them by the eternal all-necessitating decree of

God, an absolute impossibility? If this would not be wrong in God, will any one tell us what would be? Say not that this is replying against God. First prove that God does this, and that he himself has not so constituted us, that we cannot but pronounce such a doctrine wrong, and then we will consider the charge of replying against God. I say that this doctrine cannot be true, for the obvious reason that, as God himself has constituted us, we cannot but know that such a doctrine imputes to the Most High the most flagrant form of tyranny of which the human mind can conceive.

2. The high Calvinist explanation of this verse presents Paul to our contemplation as having affirmed the doctrine of eternal and unconditional election and reprobation, and the Jew as an opposer of this same doctrine, and as bringing this objection to the *principle* of election and reprobation, that it renders it unjust in God to blame the sinner for what he does. Suppose, now, that it should turn out that the Jew himself was an advocate, and a very strenuous advocate, of this very doctrine. On the supposition that Paul had affirmed this doctrine, how could the Jew, being himself a stern predestinarian, appear as an objector against it? That the Jew was a predestinarian I will now proceed to show. The main sect of the Jews, as is well known,—the sect to which Paul belonged, and which he referred to in all his writings,— was the Pharisees. What were their views on the doctrine under consideration? "They," (the Pharisees,) says the learned Jahn, in his Biblical Archaeology, "agreed with the Stoics in teaching the doctrine of *fate*, or an immutable order of things, fixed by the *decree of God.* Perhaps it may be more agreeable to some, if we should denominate their opinions, in this respect, *the doctrine of Divine Providence,* i. e., that superintendence of the superior Being which rules and cooperates with all events in such a manner as to prevent, at least, their being left entirely dependent on the will of man, since the actions of

man himself are dependent on the eternal purpose of God. Josephus, Antiq. xiii. 5, 9, xviii. 1, 3, Jewish War ii. 8, 14." How could the Calvinistic doctrine of predestination be more correctly stated than it is in the above extract, containing the doctrine as held by the Pharisees? That they did hold this doctrine in this very form, I will now show by citing one of the passages referred to in Josephus. "They," (the Pharisees,) says Josephus, Jewish Wars ii. 8, 14, "ascribe all to fate, (or Providence,) and to God; and yet allow that to act right, or the contrary, is principally in the power of man; although fate does cooperate in every action." If, then, Paul held and taught the doctrine of unconditional election and reprobation, there could have been no difference between him and the Jew, as far as the principle of election and reprobation is concerned. The only question that could have arisen, would have pertained to this one, who are the elect and who are the reprobate? In respect to the principle itself, there would have been a perfect agreement between them. But the Calvinistic explanation of the verse under consideration presents the Jew as an objector to the principle or doctrine itself, and not to PAUL'S view of its applications. This explanation, then, cannot be the true one. Paul, in the declaration "Thou wilt say then unto me, Why doth he yet find fault: for who hath resisted his will?" does not present himself as having previously affirmed the doctrine of eternal and unconditional election, and the Jew as an objector to this doctrine; for the Jew, as a matter of fact, was not an objector to it, but an advocate of it. Some other explanation, then, must be sought of the verse under consideration. This leads me to inquire—

3. After the real explanation. What does a wicked man, holding the doctrine of predestination, always do, when pressed with a conviction of obligation to do or admit what he is unwilling to do or admit? He always falls back, in self-justification, upon his own doctrine. This is, and

ever has been, his invariable resort. Why do you blame me? is his reply. How can I help being what I am, or doing what I do? A conscientious predestinarian will not do this. But a wicked man, such as the reprobate Jew, to whom Paul was writing, was, always does it. This, then, is the real meaning of this much perverted saying of inspiration. The principle which the apostle had established, is this. The destiny of man turns wholly, not as the Jew maintained, upon patriarchal descent, but upon moral character, an acceptance or rejection of God's "righteousness." When pressed with unanswerable arguments in favor of this great truth, the Jew, in self-justification, falls back upon his own, not Paul's, doctrine of predestination. "Why do you pretend," he exclaims, "that I, as a sinner, deserve perdition? My actions are all predetermined by the irresistible will of God. I have never done anything opposed to God's will or eternal purpose." The Jew, then, I repeat, is not objecting to the doctrine of predestination, stated by Paul; but, on the other hand, to shield his conscience against the point of Paul's irresistible argument in favor of a doctrine denied by the Jew, the latter falls back, in self-defence, upon his own doctrine of predestination. I know, is the language of Paul to him, what you will do, under the pressure of my argument, that the destiny of men depends not upon patriarchal descent, in other words, upon fate, or the eternal decree of God, as must be true; according to the doctrine of the Jew, but upon moral character, or acceptance, or rejection, of God's righteousness. You will fall back, as a last resort, upon your own doctrine of predestination.

In the early part of the epistle the Jew is represented as resorting, in similar manner, to his own predestination, to shield himself from the pressure of the apostle's argument on the doctrine of justification. In the second chapter, the apostle lays down the doctrine that the destiny of men turns wholly upon one principle—moral character.

"Who will render to every man according to his deeds: to them who, by patient continuance in well doing, seek for glory and honor and immortality, eternal life; but unto those that are contentious, and do not obey the truth, but obey unrighteousness, indignation and wrath, tribulation and anguish, upon every soul of man that doeth evil, of the Jew first, and also of the Gentile."

The cavil of the Jew against this doctrine, and Paul's demonstrations of its truth, and that under the influence of his ideas of predestinarianism, we meet with in the next chapter. "What," he exclaims, "if some (of the Jews) did not believe? shall their unbelief make the faith of God without effect?" God has promised to save our nation, is the argument of the Jew, and shall sin in us prevent God fulfilling that promise? Paul admits that God will be true, though all men be found liars. He then cites a passage to prove that a Jew may deserve eternal death and can escape it only by repentance and faith in God's mercy, both of which are implied in David's confession. "God forbid; yea, let God be true, but every man a liar; as it is written, That thou mightest be justified in thy sayings, and mightest overcome when thou art judged. But if our unrighteousness commend the righteousness of God, what shall we say then?" continues the cavilling Jew, under the influence of his own predestinarianism. "Is God," or rather, as Mr. Barnes shows it should be rendered, "Is not God unrighteous who taketh vengeance?" That is, if we should continue in sin, and God, according to his promise, saves us, then our sin would render God's faithfulness to his promise the more conspicuous: how, then, could God properly take vengeance on me?" "I speak as a man," says the apostle, that is, I present the cavil, just as the reprobate Jew, under the influence of his own idea of predestination, is accustomed to do it. "God forbid," replies the apostle; "how, then, shall God judge the world?" The Jew admitted that he would do this, but had just presented a cavil which, if admitted, would render such judgment unjust. "For if the truth of God hath more abounded through my lie unto his glory, why yet am I also judged as a sinner?" To this predestinarian cavil, the apostle replies by asking the Jew why he does not push his principle to its legitimate consequences, and say, as some slanderously reported that even the Christians, identifying them with the Jews, did say, "let us do evil that good may come." Here we have a striking example of the resort of all wicked men who hold the doctrine of predestination, when pressed upon in any direction whatever. They always fall back, in sell-justification, upon the doctrine of decrees. Paul has said nothing in the second chapter to occasion the predestinarian cavil which we meet with in the third. Nor has he said anything in the ninth, to give rise to the same cavil which we meet with in the verse under consideration. The common error, in the explanation of this verse, is this: Paul, it is supposed, must have previously taught some doctrine which would naturally give rise to this objection; and, as no doctrine conceivable could do this but that of decrees, that must have been the doctrine affirmed in the prior part of the chapter. The truth of the case is this. Neither in chapter second, nor in chapter nine, (for he has asserted the same in both,) has he said any such thing. In both alike, however, the Jew falls back, in self-justification, upon his own doctrine of predestination. The true meaning of the verse, then, is this. I know well the cavil that you will present against all appeals to your conscience in opposition to any form of error which you hold. You will fall back upon your own doctrine of irresistible fate or decrees, and deny that God has any right, inasmuch as his will irresistibly determines all your actions, to blame you at all.

Such is the cavil of the Jew expressed in verse 19. This cavil the apostle meets, or rather rebukes, by putting four important questions to the caviller. In the first, he charges him with the impiety of replying against God. The Jew himself admitted the divine authority of the Scriptures. For him, then, when confronted with their plain and positive declarations, the meaning of which he could neither mistake nor deny,—for him, then, to throw himself back upon his own sentiments, and on their authority to deny his desert of judgments which he could not deny that God himself had threatened to inflict, was certainly to be guilty of replying against God; it was the same as for the "thing formed to say to him that formed it, Why hast thou made me thus?" Paul had shown the Jew, from his own divinely acknowledged Scriptures, that God had made him a moral agent, and would deal with him as such. Against this great fundamental principle of the divine government, the Jew urged his predestinarian cavils. This, certainly, was for "the thing formed to say to him that formed it, Why hast thou made me thus?" Such flagrant impiety the apostle rebukes, in the most withering terms, in the two questions contained in verse 20: "Nay, but, O man, who art thou that repliest against God? Shall the thing formed say to him that formed *it,* Why hast thou made me thus?" According to the high Calvinist's explanation of this passage, the Jew replies against God, by objecting to the doctrine of predestination established by Paul, that it destroys human accountability. According to the true explanation, he replies against God, by denying the doctrine of moral agency and accountability, proved, by Paul, by an appeal to the Jewish Scriptures, and denying this great fundamental principle of God's eternal government, on the authority of his own predestinarianism. According to the high Calvinist's explanation, "the thing formed says to him that formed it, Why hast thou made me thus?" by affirming that the doctrine of eternal and unconditional election and reprobation, maintained by Paul, destroys human accountability. According to the true explanation, "the thing formed" perpetrates this horrid impiety, by denying the moral agency of man and the doctrine of human accountability, on the authority of a self-assumed predestinarianism.

Verse 21 next claims our attention. "Hath not the potter power over the clay, of the same lump to make one vessel unto honor, and another unto dishonor?" In this verse, the apostle rebukes the impiety of the Jew in the cavil under consideration, and proves the reasonableness of his own doctrine, by a direct appeal to the consciousness of the Jew himself. That the apostle, in this illustration, refers to Jer. xviii. 1—10, designing thereby to keep the eye of the Jew upon his own Scriptures, and thus, if possible, silence his cavils, no one can doubt. To obtain a correct view of his real meaning, then, we must recur to the original passage itself. "The word which came to Jeremiah from the LORD, saying, Arise, and go down to the potter's house, and there I will cause thee to hear my words. Then I went down to the potter's house, and behold he wrought a work on the wheels. And the vessel that he had made of clay was marred in the hand of the potter: so he made it again another vessel, as seemed good to the potter to make *it*. Then the word of the LORD came to me, saying, O house of Israel, cannot I do with you as this potter? saith the LORD. Behold, as the clay *is* in the potter's hands, so *are* ye in mine hand, O house of Israel. *At what* instant I shall speak concerning a nation, and concerning a kingdom, to pluck up, and to pull down, and to destroy *it;* if that nation, against whom I have pronounced, turn from their evil, I will repent of the evil that I thought to do unto them. And *at what* instant I shall speak concerning a nation, and concerning a kingdom, to build and to plant *it;* if it do evil in my sight, that it obey not my voice, then I will repent of the good wherewith I said I would benefit them." In what sense are nations, and, consequently, individuals, in the hands of God, as the clay is in those of the potter, according to this passage? Is it in this sense, as the high Calvinist affirms, that God claims the prerogative of rendering, by his own resistless agency, the character of one holy and the other sinful, and then, saving the one and destroying the other, for becoming what he himself has rendered it impossible for them not to become? A more false and impious construction cannot possibly be put upon the passage. This, on the other hand, is the true explanation. As the potter, after mingling his clay, claims the right to mould its diverse parts into vessels of honor or dishonor, as shall suit his purposes; so God, after doing all he wisely can to render all pure and holy, and thus fitting them to become vessels of honor, claims the sovereign prerogative, should he still find a part of them sinful and a part holy, to select his vessels of honor and dishonor accordingly, and that, wholly independent of any external relations whatever. In this sense, and in this only, are we, according to this passage, in God's hands, as the clay in the hands of the potter. That this is the very doctrine maintained by Paul in the verse under consideration, is perfectly evident—1. From the fact that such, as we have seen, is the undeniable meaning of the passage in the Old Testament, from which he takes his illustration. 2. This was the point, and in truth the only point, at issue between him and the Jew. The question which Paul is debating with the Jew, is whether God has a right to make moral character, when formed, the basis of his treatment of men, and reward or punish Jew or Gentile according to character, irrespective of all other considerations. The Jew affirmed that all Jews, whatever their character, must be formed into vessels of mercy, and all Gentiles into vessels of wrath. God had no right, of the same mass, however diverse in character, to make one vessel unto honor and another unto dishonor. The apostle maintained the opposite doctrine. Here, and on this point only, as far as the present chapter is concerned, does he join issue with the Jew. We must understand the apostle, then, as using the illustration of the potter and clay for this purpose exclusively. 3. The nature of the apostle's illustration shows that this is his meaning. The original term here rendered "lump," does not mean the clay as first taken from the bed, but after it has been mingled and ready to be placed on the wheel to be formed into vessels. Where it is said, John ix. 6, that "Christ spat on the ground and made clay of the spittle," the word there rendered "clay" is the same as the one here rendered "lump." The figure, then, is not at all adapted to express the high Calvinistic notion, of first moulding character, and then awarding and punishing accordingly; but that of treating—creatures, after character has been consummated, according to their respective deserts. In this sense, then, and in this only, are we, according to this passage, in the hands of God, as clay in the hands of the potter. The question put to the Jew, then, is this—Has not God the same right to treat men according to their moral deserts, and that whether Jew or Gentile, that the potter has of the same mass of clay to make one vessel unto honor and another unto dishonor?[4]

---

[4] "I saw from the inspired application and interpretation of the action which the prophet witnessed in the potter's house, that what to a superficial reader appears to be the meaning of the passage, is not its real meaning; I saw that it contained a meaning not only different from, but opposed to, the ordinary doctrine of election: for it declared that the future prospects of men were placed by God in their own hands; and that, as God's promises and threatenings were addressed not to individuals but to characters, a man, by chancing his character, might change God's dealing towards him. I saw that it was adduced for the purpose of maintaining, not that the potter had a right to make a vessel good or bad according to his own pleasure, but that he had a right, if a vessel turned out ill in his hands, to reject that vessel, and break it down, and make it up anew into another vessel. The right of making a thing bad is not contemplated at all in the passage; the matter considered is, whether the potter, after having once made a vessel, is bound to preserve it, although it turns out

Verses 22—24 now admit of a ready explanation. In the preceding part of the epistle, as well as in this particular chapter, the apostle had established the following truths: 1. God is determined, if men will not repent, after all his efforts to secure it, to show his wrath against sin, and make his power to punish it known in their destruction. "Indignation and wrath upon every soul of man that doeth evil, to the Jew first, and also to the Gentile." 2. To prevent such a consummation, he endures with much long-suffering with sinners, even though, in their character, they are "vessels of wrath fitted to destruction:" "the goodness of God leadeth them to repentance." 3. He endures this for the purpose of rendering them fitted to become vessels of mercy, and then making known upon them, as such, "the riches of his glory." "But glory, honor, and peace, to every man that doeth good, to the Jew first, and also to the Gentile." All these great truths the apostle blends together into this one passage, and asks the Jew what he has to object, on the supposition that God treats men according to these principles. "What (that is, what have you to object) if God, willing (being determined) to show his wrath, and to make his power known, (in case sinners will not turn from their sins,) endured (to prevent their destruction) with much long-suffering the vessels of wrath fitted to destruction," and thus endured them, that, on their becoming fit to be rendered vessels of mercy, "he might make known the riches of his glory on the vessels of mercy, whom he had afore (before

---

quite unfit for the purpose for which it was made: or whether, in such a case, he has the right of rejecting it. And as the exercise of the right of rejection on the part of the potter is unquestioned, ALTHROUGH HIS WORKS DO NOT GO WRONG BY THEIR OWN FAULT, much more does God claim to himself the right of rejecting a people whom he had set up for a particular purpose, *if they refused to answer that purpose.*"—*Thomas Erskine, Esq., Advocate.*

admitting them to life) prepared unto glory, even us, whom he hath called, not of the Jews only, but also of the Gentiles?" What, the Jew is asked, can he object, if God, after having done all he wisely can to render all alike fit to be made vessels of mercy, treats Jews and Gentiles according to their character thus formed? And who, in the wide universe, can object to such principles of administration as these? But suppose that God first determines, past the possibility of change or modification, what the character of men shall be, and then saves a part and dooms the rest to the endurance of his eternal wrath, for being what, and not otherwise, than he himself rendered it impossible for them not to become? What must be the verdict of the universal conscience in respect to the character of such an administration? How is it possible for a being, perfectly wise and righteous, to be filled with eternal "indignation and wrath," against creatures, for simply becoming what he himself rendered it impossible for them not to become? Can you, reader, show that this is possible?

REMARKS.

1. The fundamental error in the high Calvinist explanation of Romans ix. now becomes perfectly manifest. That explanation rests wholly upon this one assumption, and can be sustained on no other, to wit, that Paul throughout the chapter, as a predestinarian, is arguing with the Jew as an anti-predestinarian. This assumption is the basis of this explanation of all the most material verses of the chanter. In v. 16, "It is not of him that willeth," &c., the Calvinistic explanation makes Paul, as a predestinarian, affirm that conversion, and consequently salvation, in no sense depend on the will of man, but wholly upon the sovereign, irresistible will of God, and presents the Jew as an anti-predestinarian, affirming that conversion, and consequently final salvation or destruction do depend upon the will or choice of man. The Calvinistic explanation makes Paul, as a predestinarian, affirm, in verse 18,

"Therefore, hath he mercy," &c., that God, in the fulfilment of an eternal, all-necessitating decree, makes men sinful or holy according to his own sovereign pleasure; and presents the Jew, as an anti-predestinarian, as denying this doctrine. The explanation under consideration makes the Jew, in v. 19, "Thou will say unto me, Why doth he yet find fault?" &c., as an anti-predestinarian, object to the doctrine of predestination on the ground that it destroys human accountability; and presents Paul, in the verse following, as a predestinarian, charging the Jew, with replying against God, in thus objecting to this doctrine. The high Calvinist explanation can, by no possibility, be sustained on any other supposition. Now, such an opposition never could have existed, if Paul himself was a predestinarian, and argued with the Jew as such. The Jew, himself a high predestinarian, could not have been at issue with Paul, as the high Calvinist explanation makes him, in respect to the doctrine itself. He could have differed with him only in respect to the *application* of the doctrine. Paul, knowing as he could not but have done, the real sentiments of the Jew, would have been a dishonest man, had he presented the Jew, as the Calvinistic explanation makes him present his countrymen, as opposed to the doctrine of predestination.

2. Here, also, I notice a common mistake in reference to the relations of Christ and his apostles, and the Primitive Church to the world, as far as the doctrine of necessity and predestination is concerned. The common impression is, that they went everywhere preaching this doctrine, and that the world arrayed itself in opposition to them in reference to it. Now, no such opposition did or could have existed; for the obvious reason that all the world, as a matter of fact, with almost no exceptions, held the doctrine of necessity, and stood opposed to that of free-will. The Primitive Church, as it came out from under the direct teachings of Christ and his apostles, stood in unbroken columns in opposition to the opinions of the world in reference to these doctrines. In other words, the Primitive Church, with one voice, stood before the world in opposition to the Calvinistic doctrine of predestination, and

in favor of the opposite doctrine. To show this, I will now present the following extract from a work of my own on the Will:—

"But the testimony of the early Christian fathers themselves leaves no doubt upon this point. I will cite the declarations of a few of them. 'If it happen by fate,' (or necessity,) says Justin Martyr, who lived in the second century, 'that men were either good or wicked, the good were not good, nor should the wicked be wicked.' In another place he says, 'Every created being is so constituted as to be capable of vice and virtue. For he can do nothing praiseworthy, if he had not the power of turning either way.' Again, he says, 'Unless we suppose man has the power to choose the good and refuse the evil, no one can be accountable for any action whatever.' Once more: 'God has not made man, like trees and brutes, without the power of election.' 'No reward,' says Tertullian, who flourished in the same century, 'can justly be bestowed, no punishment can justly be inflicted, upon him who is good or bad by necessity, and not by his own choice.' Again he says, that 'Man being appointed for God's judgment, it was necessary to the justice of God's sentence, that man should be judged according to the deserts of his free-will.'

"Irenaeus, bishop of Lyons, and of the same century, says, 'Man, a reasonable being, and in that respect like God, is made free in his will, and having, power over himself, is the cause that sometimes he becomes wheat and sometimes chaff.' Again: 'They who do good shall obtain honor and glory, because they have done good when they could forbear doing it. And they who do it not, shall receive just judgment of our God, because they have not done good when they could have done it.' 'What is forced,' says Basil, one of the most distinguished of the ancient fathers, 'is not pleasing to God, but what comes from a purely virtuous motive; and virtue comes from the will, not from necessity.' Again: 'The will depends on what is within us, and within us is free-will.'

"'Forasmuch as God has put good and evil in our own power,' says Chrysostom, 'he has given us a free power to choose one or the other; and, as he does not retain us against our will, so he embraces us when we are willing.' Again: 'After a wicked man, if he will, is changed into a good man, and a good man, through sloth, falls away and becomes wicked; because God hath endowed us with free agency; nor does he make us to do things necessarily, but he places proper remedies before us, and suffers all to be done according to the will of the patient.'

"'God,' says Jerome, 'hath endowed us with freewill. We are not necessarily drawn either to virtue or sin. For when necessity rules, there is no room left either for damnation or the crown.' Again: 'Even to those who shall be wicked, God gives power to repent and turn him.' In another place, be says 'Our will is kept free to turn either way, that God may dispense his rewards and punishments, not according to his own pre-judgment, but according to the merits of every one.' Once more: 'Let him who condemns it (free will) be himself condemned.'

"'It would be more just,' says Epiphanius, 'to punish the stars, which make a wicked action necessary,' (this was said in reference to the heathen notion that the stars determine destiny,) 'than to punish the poor man, who does that wicked action by necessity.'

"'The soul,' says Origen, 'does not incline to either part out of necessity, for then neither vice nor virtue could be ascribed to it; not would its choice of virtue deserve reward; nor its declination to vice, punishment.' Again: 'How could God require that of man, which he (man) had not power to offer him?'

"'Ten thousand things,' says Theodoret, 'may be found, both in the gospels and authorities of the apostles, clearly manifesting the liberty and self-election of man.' Again, 'For how can he (God) punish a nature (with endless torments) which had no power to do good, but was bound in the bands of wickedness?'

"'Neither promises nor reprehensions, rewards nor punishments, are just,' says Clemens of Alexandria, 'if the soul has not the power of choosing or abstaining; but evil is involuntary,' that is, necessary. Eusebius, of the fourth century, declares, that 'This opinion,' the doctrine of fate or necessity, 'absolves sinners, as doing nothing of their own accord, which was evil; and would cast all the blame of all wickedness committed in the world, upon God and upon his Providence.'

"Didymue, also of the fourth century, after asserting the doctrine of liberty, says, 'And this is not only ours, but the opinion of all those who speak orthodoxly (according to the opinion of tire Universal Church) of rational beings.'

"Even Augustine—the first necessitarian, I believe, known in the church—is often constrained by the force of the universal opinion of the church, in his own and the preceding ages, to assert, though in strange inconsistency with himself, the doctrine of liberty, 'They that come to Christ,' he says, 'ought not to impute it to themselves, because they come, being called; and they that would not come, ought not to impute it to another, but only to themselves, because, when they are called, it was in the power of their free will to come.'"

3. In the portion of this chapter which has occupied our attention in the present lecture, God is represented as exercising great forbearance and long-suffering towards all sinners. Of the object of such forbearance we are most clearly informed in other parts of the Bible. It is the actual salvation of the sinner. According to the high Calvinist doctrine, forbearance can never be exercised towards the non-elect for any such end; because that, in conformity to a sovereign eternal decree of God, they are left in circumstance in which their salvation is an absolute impossibility. Nor does the lengthening out of life serve any purpose, so far as they are concerned, but to increase their guilt and consequent wretchedness to eternity. To call this forbearance and long-suffering, is to reverse all the ideas which such words are adapted and designed to convey. If this doctrine is true, forbearance and

long-suffering can have no place in God's treatment of the non-elect. They can have been brought into being, and their so-called probation can be lengthened out, for no other purpose, as far as they, as individuals, are concerned, but their eternal damnation, and that in its most aggravated form; the very reverse of all God's designs and intentions in respect to them, according to the express teachings of the Scriptures.

LECTURE IV.
Verses 25—33.
GENERAL RECAPITULATION.

A SHORT recapitulation of the apostle's argument, from the commencement of this chapter to the close of verse 24, may be expedient, as introductory to the explanation of the remaining portion which is to occupy our attention in this lecture. In the first five verses the apostle protests, in the most solemn manner, his sorrow, for his brethren the Jews, in view of their impending doom, consequent on their rejection of God's righteousness, which is through faith alone in Christ Jesus. In the same connection, the apostle enumerates certain important privileges which pertained to the Jew consequent on his relations to the patriarchs, as the messianic seed of Abraham; privileges in which the Jew was accustomed to glory, and on which he rested his hope of eternal life; privileges, however, the thought of which tended only to aggravate the sorrow of the apostle, attended as it was with the melancholy reflection, that a people thus privileged should finally be lost, and as a consequence suffer a doom of corresponding aggravation. The apostle, then, verse 6, states the proposition which it is his exclusive object to elucidate and establish in the remaining portion of the chapter. The Jew supposed that whatever threatenings were denounced against sinners in the Scriptures, he was perfectly secure against them, however he might live himself; for the reason, that his salvation did not turn upon his moral character at all, but upon his patriarchal descent. "Not as though the word of God hath taken none effect," is the proposition which the apostle lays down in opposition to this fundamental error of his countrymen; that is, the case of the Jew, consequent on all the privileges pertaining to him on account of his patriarchal descent, is not, as he vainly supposes, such that the word of God's threatening has become ineffectual, or lost its curse-inflicting power in respect to him, any more than in respect to other sinners, and this for the reason, that "all are not (as the Jew supposes) Israel (heirs with Israel of life eternal) who are of Israel, (lineally descended from Israel;) neither because they are the seed (lineal descendants) of Abraham are they all children," that is, spiritually so.

To substantiate this proposition, the apostle (verses 8—13) cites the cases of the descendants of Ishmael and Easu. In respect to them, the Jew himself acknowledged, 1. That they were the real descendants of Abraham. 2. That patriarchal descent did not avail, in their case, to place them even among the messianic seed of Abraham, much less secure for them a place among his spiritual children. How obvious, then, is the conclusion, that mere patriarchal descent does not secure an individual a place among "the children of God;" and how presumptuous in the Jew, to suppose that because he was merely lineally descended from Abraham, he was therefore secure, whatever his character might be, against God's word of threatening, and an heir with Abraham of life eternal!

To show that suspending the destiny of man, not upon patriarchal descent, but upon an acceptance or rejection of God's righteousness, does not imply that there is "unrighteousness with God," the apostle makes (verses 14—18) a direct appeal in the Scriptures, the divine authority of which the Jew himself acknowledged. The first passage cited is the declaration of God to Moses, consequent on the prayer of Moses that God would pardon Jews who had sinned, and were still impenitent. God refuses to answer the request, saying, "I will have mercy on whom I will have mercy, and will have compassion no whom I will have compassion;" that is, my principles for dispensing pardon are fixed and changeless; the prayer of no individual, in behalf of any who refuse to comply with the condition which I have laid down, will avail at all to change my purpose in respect to this subject. Hence, the apostle infers (verse 16) that the *condition* of mercy dose not depend upon the will of him that seeks it, nor upon that of him who uses means to obtain it, but upon the will of God who is to bestow it, "So, then, *it is* not of him that willeth, nor of him that runneth, but of God that showeth mercy." The Jew, then, if he would escape God's word of threatening, and become a subject of divine mercy, should not, as he was doing, go about to establish his own righteousness, and thus prescribe for God the condition of mercy. On the other hand, he should go to God, and learn from him what his condition is; and, by humble compliance, render his own "calling and elective sure."

In verse 17, the apostle cites, in further confirmation of his position, against the error of the Jew, the declaration of God to Pharaoh,—a declaration in which the Most High avows the great fact, in the first instance, that he had raised Pharaoh up from the fearful diseases from which he had just been restored, for the purpose of "showing him the divine power," and that as a means of his salvation; and then, in the next instance, declares that his ultimate design in respect to him, was, through him as a monument of mercy if he did repent, or a monument of wrath if he continued to harden himself against God, to bring about a consummation, in which, for the salvation of the race, "God's name should be declared throughout all the earth." "For the Scripture saith unto Pharaoh, even for this same purpose have I raised thee up, that I might show my power in thee, and that my name might be declared throughout all the earth." From the undeniable fact, that God refused to pardon the impenitent Jew, even when Moses prayed for it, and avowed the purpose to pardon and save even Pharaoh, if he would repent, and finally destroyed him, only when he had hardened himself into incurable reprobacy, how evident is the conclusion which the apostle draws, (verse 18,) that God is not, as the Jew supposed, confined to the principle of patriarchal descent, in selecting his vessels of mercy or of judgment; but that, on the other hand, according to his own divinely prescribed principle, in conformity to which he is merciful towards, or pardons, those who humbly "submit themselves, to the righteousness of God," and is hard or relentless towards, that is, inflicts his word of threatening upon all those who harden themselves against him, that "therefore hath he mercy on whom he will have mercy, and whom he will he hardeneth."

The apostle was well aware of what would be the final resort of the Jew, in self-defence, against appeals to his own Scriptures, appeals to which he could make no reply. As a stern, high predestinarian, and being at the same time devoid of moral principle, he would fall back as he had done (chap, iii, ver. 1—8) to shield himself against the apostle's demonstration of the doctrine of justification by faith, in opposition to the Jewish error of salvation by deeds of law; he would fall back, I say, upon his own predestinarianism, and deny the fact of his own guilt and consequent desert of punishment. As making such an impious reply to his arguments, the apostle meets the Jew, (verse 19,) "Thou wilt say then unto me, Why doth he yet find fault! for who hath resisted his will?" That is, I am well aware of your last resort against appeals to your own Scripture, appeals which you cannot misunderstand or reply to. You will fall back, as you are wont to do on all other occasions, when thus sorely pressed; you will fall back again upon you own error of eternal and all-necessitating predestination, and deny the fact of your real desert of punishment. In reply, the apostle first informs the Jew that in thus refusing to yield to the undeniable teachings of his own acknowledged divinely inspired Scriptures, he stands self-convicted, in the first instance, of replying against God—a fearful attitude for a creature to assume in respect to his Creator. In denying the fact of his moral agency as he had done, in affirming the impossibility of his own desert of punishment, when God had asserted the fact that he was a moral agent, in the revelation of the great principle of His eternal government, that He would dispense mercy and judgment upon the exclusive principle of personal character, ("who will render to every man according to his deeds,") the Jew was guilty of the horrid impiety of denying the right of God to create him as he had done. "Nay, but, oh man, who art thou that repliest against God? Shall the thing formed say to him that formed it, Why hast thou made me thus?"

Still further; as God had revealed the fact (Jer, viii. 1—10) that nations and individuals are in his hands, to deal with them, as a righteous moral governor, according to their moral conduct, as the clay is in the hands of the potter, for the Jew to deny God's right to dispense mercy and judgment to Jews and Gentiles alike, accordingly as they accept or reject God's righteousness, was not only unscriptural but as absurd in itself, as it would be to affirm that the potter has not the right, of the same lump of clay, to make one vessel unto honor and another unto dishonor. "Hath not the potter power over the clay, of the same lump to make one vessel unto honor, and another unto dishonor?"

Finally; what objection could be brought against this doctrine, when it revealed God as dealing with men, whether Jews or Gentiles, upon such principles as these? 1. He is determined, in case men will remain incorrigible in their sins, to make his wrath against sin and his power to punish it known, in their destruction, 2. To prevent such a doom, he "endures with much long-suffering" the rebellion of those even who are in their character vessels of wrath fitted to destruction. 3. He thus endures them, that, on their becoming vessels of mercy, he may make known upon them as such "the riches of his glory," whether they be Jews or Gentiles. What objection could the Jew bring against a system of divine administration based wholly upon such principles? This is the meaning of the question propounded in verses 22—24. "What if God, willing to show his wrath, and to make his power known, endured with much long-suffering the vessels of wrath fitted to destruction; and that he might make known the riches of his glory on the vessels of mercy, which he had afore prepared unto glory, even us, whom he hath called, not of the Jews only, but also of the Gentiles?"

Explanation of Romans ix. 25—33,

We now advance to a direct consideration of the portion of the chapter which is to be the subject of attention in this lecture. In respect to this part of the chapter there is, happily, but a very little diversity of opinion among commentators. It naturally divides itself into two parts. In the first, including verses 25—28, the apostle proves, by a direct appeal to Scripture, that Gentile believers are to constitute a portion of the church or elect of God, and that not all, as the Jew maintained, but a part only of the Jews will be saved; thus disproving the two great errors of the Jew, to wit, that sin in him will not expose him to the curse revealed in God's word of threatening, and that faith in the Gentile will not secure him a place among the children of God. In the second part of this passage, (verses 29—33,) the apostle presents the great and conclusive reason why the Jew had failed to attain the righteousness which he sought. We will consider these portions of the passage separately.

In verse 25, the apostle makes a quotation from Hosea i. 10, and quotes the passage not literally, but according to its real import. In this passage the great truth stands directly and distinctly revealed, that Gentiles were to become a constituent portion of the Church of Christ, Gentiles of no class, up to that time, had been called God's people; but now such of them as believe were to be called his people. They had never had a place among the people who were called God's beloved; but now they were to wear this endearing title, "As he saith also in Osee, I will call them my people, which were not my people; and her beloved, which was not beloved." Thus the error of the Jew, that the Gentile, though a believer, cannot be saved, was made manifest.

Verse 26 has an exclusive reference to the Jews. To understand it, we must refer to the whole passage from which it was originally taken; to wit, Hosea i. 8—10: "Now when she had weaned Lo-ruhamah, she conceived and bare a son. Then said God, Call his name Lo-ammi; for ye are not my people, and I will not be your God. Yet the number of the children of Israel shall be as the sand of the sea, which cannot be measured nor numbered; and it shall come to pass, that in the place where it was said unto them, Ye are not my people, there it shall be said unto them, Ye are the sons of the living God." The term Lo-ammi means Not-my-people. The daughter which the wife of the prophet had previously borne he was directed to call Lo-ammi, Not-my-people; because the Jews, who had before been called Ammi, My-people, were, in the fulfilment of this prophecy, to cease to be called such. They were to be called Lo-ammi, Not-my-people, because they were to be cut off for their wickedness from that peculiar relation to God. Yet the time would come, in the progress of ages, when their "number would be as the sands of the sea, and in the very place where it was said unto them, Ye are not my people, there it shall be said unto them, Ye are the sons of the living God." This passage, then, contains the following truths respecting the Jews. 1. The time would come when they would cease to stand before the world as the acknowledged people of God. God himself would reject them for their sins. 2. In the progress of subsequent ages they would—their number then being immensely great—be restored to their former relations as the people of God. This passage, then, clearly demonstrates the truth of the great proposition stated in verse 6, that the Jew, consequent on his patriarchal decent, is not curse-proof against God's word of threatening. This, as I suppose, must be the object of the apostle in citing from Hosea the passage under consideration.

Some have supposed that both passages above cited relate to the Gentiles, placing what follows, as quoted from Isaiah, concerning the Jews, in contrast with what is said in Hosea, concerning the Gentiles. No difference in the bearing of the whole upon the apostle's argument is made, whichever way the passages are explained. To my mind, however, the above is obviously the true explanation.

Of the meaning of the following verse, 27—29, there can be no doubt. In verse 27, quoted from Isaiah x. 22, it is affirmed that, although the number of the people of Israel was immensely great, such an idea being properly expressed by the figure, "as the sand of the sea," "a remnant" only would escape destruction. This implied that the mass of the people would perish in their sins, and, consequently, demonstrated the truth of the proposition which it was the great object of the apostle to establish, to wit, that the Jew, was not secure against God's word of threatening. Such is the meaning of the words "Esaias also crieth concerning Israel, Though the number of the children of Israel be as the sand of the sea, a remnant shall be saved."

Verse 28 is immediately connected with the one just explained, and constitutes a part of Isaiah x. 22, and the whole of the following verse. Its meaning has been expressed in a former lecture, and may be thus expressed: "For,"—that is, what I have said will surely take place, or "I speak of the remnant only, for a different destiny awaits the rest, or the mass of the people,"—"he will finish the work," (word,) or execute his word of threatening against the body of the people, "and cut it short in righteousness;" that is, execute it speedily in righteousness;" that is, execute it speedily in righteous vengeance: "because a short work (word) will the Lord make in the earth;" that is, God will cause his word of threatening to be shortly or speedily executed in the sight of the whole earth. The meaning of the two verses, taken together, may be thus expressed: "Though the number of the children of Israel be now immensely great, but a remnant of them shall escape the judgments impending over them; for God will accomplish this threatening upon the mass of the nation, and bring that threatening to a speedy consummation. Most assuredly will God cause his word of threatening to be speedily consummated in the sight of the whole earth." In the presence of such fearful declarations pertaining to the Jewish nation, how presumptuous in the Jew to entertain the idea that he, in consequence of his patriarchal decent, is curse-proof in respect to God's threatened judgments upon all who "reject his great salvation!"

In verse 29 the apostle confirms what he had proved in the verses preceding, by another quotation from Isa. i. 9. "And as Esaias said before, (in a former chapter,) Except the Lord of Sabaoth (of hosts) had left us a seed, (a remnant or portion surviving, this being the meaning of the term seed,) we had been as Sodom, and been made like unto Gomorrah;" that is, our nation would have utterly perished. Thus the apostle proved, by a direct appeal to the Scriptures, that the divine dispensation hung over the Jew and Gentile alike, filled with vials of mercy and vials of wrath, and that neither could enjoy the one or shun the other, unless on one condition, "submission to God's righteousness."

The connection between the opposite quotations, which the apostle makes from the prophets Hosea and Isaiah, concerning the Jews, is very striking. Hosea points to a consummation in the progress of the nation, in which, after they have been for ages Lo-ammi, they should become, their numbering immensely great, Ammi, or "the sons of the living God." But Isaiah points to a prior consummation of a different kind, when their number, at the time, being indeed immense, yet only a remnant would escape the judgments of God. Both quotations culminate in one great truth, to wit, that the Jew is not, as he supposes, in consequence of his relations and privileges as a descendant of Abraham, shielded, while he remains in his sins, from the threatened judgments of God.

The above quotation, also, in the same manner as the apostle's entire course of reasoning throughout, shows clearly that I have rightly explained his meaning in the phrase, verse 6, "not as thought the word of God hath taken none effect," in explaining the phrase "the word of God" to mean, not his word of promise, but his word of threatening. The reasonings and quotations of the apostle everywhere bear directly and immediately upon this latter idea, and not so directly and immediately upon the former. We may very safely and assuredly conclude, then, that that phrase has been rightly explained, as well as the train of argumentation pursued to establish it.

The apostle has now completed his demonstration of the proposition before us, and proceeds, in the remainder of the chapter, to introduce another and different subject,—a subject, however, not disconnected with the one which has previously occupied our attention. Two facts were undeniable: that portion of the Gentiles, while they had, prior to the proclamation of God's righteousness, which is through faith in Christ alone, made no efforts at all for their own salvation, had now attained to this righteousness; while the mass of the Jews, although they had attempted to attain to a certain form of righteousness, had failed of attaining to any form of real righteousness whatever. To announce this fact, and to state the reason of the total failure of the Jew, is the object of the apostle in the remaining part of this chapter:—"What shall we say then? That the Gentiles, which followed not after righteousness, have attained to righteousness, even the righteousness which is of faith. But Israel, which followed after the law of righteousness, hath not attained to the law of righteousness." The article "the," before the term Gentile, in the 30th verse, and before the words "law of righteousness," in the verse following, is not, in either instance, in the original, and had better have been omitted in the translation. The apostle does not mean to say that "the Gentiles," that is, the mass of them, but the "Gentiles," that is, a certain portion of them, had attained to the righteousness referred to. Nor does he intend to say that the Jews, who rejected Christ, had followed after "the law," that is, the true law of righteousness. On the other hand, they had followed, as the apostle shows in chapter x. 5, *a* law of righteousness, that is, a law of their own; in doing which, however, they had failed even to attain to "a law," that is, to any law of righteousness. The meaning of these two verses, then, may be thus expressed:—"What shall we say then?" that is, what are the real facts of the case pertaining to Jews and Gentiles? These are the facts:—Gentiles who, previous to the proclamation of the Gospel of Christ, had never sought after any form of righteousness, the righteousness which is by faith. But Jews, which did indeed aim to observe a law of righteousness, one of their own, had not attained to any law of righteousness whatever. Their efforts, even in the direction in which they were put forth, had been a total failure.

The question now arises, What is the *cause* of this melancholy fact pertaining to the Jew? The reason is obvious. He had sought righteousness indeed, but had refused to seek it in God's way. He had endeavored to attain salvation by attempting to observe a law of righteousness, that is, "as it were by works of law," and not by faith, which is God's revealed condition. The particle "the" should be omitted, before the term law, in this, as in the instances above mentioned. In seeking salvation in the wrong direction, he would of course refuse to take the right one, and thus stumble over the rock of salvation appointed by God for sinners to build their hopes upon. Christ is called a stone of stumbling to those who reject him, for two reasons. 1. In seeking righteousness in some other direction, they of course reject him. He becomes an object of offence to them. 2. As, when men stumble over an object, they are injured by the fall, so, in the rejection of Christ, the guilt and condemnation of sinners are infinitely enhanced. Hence, to all such, he is properly called "a stone of stumbling and rock of offence." Such is the meaning of verse 32. "Wherefore?" that is, what is the true cause of the total failure of the Jews? This is the true cause:—"Becuase *they sought it* not by faith, but as it were by the works of the law. For they stumbled at the stumblingstone."

The fact that Christ would become "a stone of stumbling and rock of offence" to some, as well as the author of eternal salvation to others, the apostle now shows, in the last verse of this chapter, by another quotation from Isaiah, referring directly and exclusively to Christ. The quotation is made up of two passages, and contains the real substance of both; to wit, Isaiah viii. 14; xxviii. 16. God represents himself as laying in the midst of the Jewish nation, here typified by the term Zion, (Jerusalem, or Zion, being then the capital of the nation, and properly used to express it,) a rock for the people to build their hopes for eternity upon. At the same time, he intimated that the rock, or his revealed plan of salvation, would, as a matter of fact, be to many a stumbling-stone and rock of offence; that is, many would reject, and take offence at, the plan of salvation revealed, and thereby increase their own condemnation. Whosoever would believe in him, however, would not be ashamed, or be disappointed in their expectations. The opposition of the Jew, therefore, to Christ, is no evidence that he is not the Son of God. The fact that he is to the Jew a rock of offence, on the other hand, only confirms the doctrine of salvation by faith revealed through him. Such is the meaning of verse 33. "As it is written, Behold, I lay in Sion a stumbling-stone and rock of offence; and whosoever believeth on him shall not be ashamed." In stating the reasons why the Jew had failed to attain righteousness, the apostle impliedly stated the reasons why Gentiles attained to righteousness, while the Jew had failed to attain it. The former, when the way of life was revealed to him, embraced the truth by faith, while the latter rejected it.

I have now completed the examination of this important chapter. If I have rightly explained it, some service has been done to the cause of truth and righteousness. If I have failed in the great argument, I trust that those who have heard me, and others who may read these thoughts, when presented to the public, will have wisdom to detect the error. I shall draw the lectures on this chapter to a close, with a few brief reflections of a general nature.

REMARKS.

I. I may be permitted here to allude to some considerations which go to confirm the general correctness of the explanation of the chapter which has been given in these lectures. Among these I notice the following:—

1. The explanation throughout accords with the universally received law of biblical criticism. I feel quite sure that it

cannot be shown that those laws have been violated in this exposition.

2. The entire argument of the apostle, according to this exposition, bears directly and most decisively upon the real question at issue between him and the Jew, to wit, Whether relationship to Abraham, such as the Jew sustained, did, in fact, render one secure from the judgments of God threatened against sinners? This is not the only question at issue between them, but the very question which, as all acknowledge, the apostle does discuss in this chapter. What higher evidence can we have that an explanation is correct than this, that, according to it, all parts of the passage are in harmony with the real and great question at issue between the parties, and with the question actually discussed in the passage itself?

3. Every particular part of the passage, every sentence, phrase, and quotation from Scripture, found in it, perfectly harmonizes, as we have seen, with this explanation. Nothing in the passage is out of place, nothing unhinges against our line of argument, as we traverse the passage from beginning to end. Such are the grounds on which I rest the claims of the explanation of Romans ix. given in these lectures.

II. The fundamental objections which lie against the high Calvinist explanation of the passage next claim our attention.

1. This explanation throughout rests upon an assumption known to be false, to wit, that Paul is here, as a predestinarian, reasoning against the Jew, as an anti-predestinarian; when, in fact, the Jew was himself a high predestinarian, and could not have been at issue with the apostle on this subject, if Paul was himself a predestinarian.

2. This explanation makes Paul lay out his *main stress* in proving points where there is no difference of opinion at all, if he was a predestinarian; instead of concentrating his whole force, as he should have done, upon the real question in difference, the question, Who were, and who were not, the elect? Can we suppose that such a man, under immediate inspiration of the Holy Spirit, would take such a course as that?

3. According to this explanation, the main direction of the apostle's reasoning is wholly apart from the point which, as all acknowledge, he was aiming to prove, and had no bearing upon it whatever. The point on which the apostle is arguing, as all admit, is the proposition that patriarchal descent does not render the Jew sure of God's favor, and safe from the threatenings which he has denounced against sinners. What adaptation has an argument to prove the doctrine of eternal and unconditional election and reprobation to settle such a proposition as this?

4. According to this explanation, the apostle's reasonings, throughout the chapter, lack the *unity* which every else characterize him as a reasoner. At one time, he is arguing the real question at issue; at another, a point where there was no difference of opinion, and that just as if such difference did exist. No such example can be found in Paul's writings anywhere else.

5. This explanation makes the apostle contradict himself in different parts of the chapter. At one time it makes him assign, as the sole reason of the destruction of the Jew, the eternal decree and sovereignty of God. "It is not of him that willeth, nor of him that runneth, but of God that showeth mercy." Then, in another place, it makes him affirm that the Jew himself is the sole cause of his own death. "Wherefore? Because they sought it not by faith." What must we think of an explanation which places different parts of the same chapter in such open opposition to each other?

6. Another fundamental objection to this explanation—an objection not yet referred to in these lectures—next claims our special attention. According to this explanation, the connection between the first five verses and the remaining portion of the chapter is the most unnatural imaginable. In these verse the apostle represents the impending doom of the Jew as a source of the greatest conceivable sorrow and grief to him. According to this explanation, he then goes on to present this very doom as occurring according to, and in consequence of, an eternal and irreversible purpose and decree

of God. No event, whatever its character in itself, can be, *when* thus contemplated, an object of continual sorrow and heart-heaviness to a truly devout, believing, submissive, and trustful mind. The moment any event whatever is contemplated by such a mind, as an object of eternal and irreversible purpose of God, it then becomes, however the mind may be affected by it when contemplated from other points of view, an object of submissive acquiescence and holy joy, and not of mental sorrow. Paul, then, as a holy man, and under the immediate inspiration of the Holy Spirit, could never have presented the doom of his countrymen as a source of "great heaviness and continual sorrow in his heart," and then, in the same connection, present the same event as the object of an eternal and irreversible purpose and decree of God. The high Calvinist's explanation, which imputes to him such inconsistency,—yes, unsubmissiveness and impiety, as such a state of mind, in such a connection, would be,— cannot be the correct interpretation. A different and opposite construction ought to be put upon the chapter.

III. A great truth, clearly brought to view in verses 30—33 of this chapter, next claims our attention. It is this. All persons who are seeking salvation in a wrong direction, and who vainly suppose themselves to have thus secured it, are, in fact, in a condition far more hopeless than those who are not seeking it at all. The individual who knows himself "without God in the world," is far more likely to take warning and "lay hold on the hope set before him."

IV. We are now prepared for a distinct consideration of the fundamental *principle*, or distinguishing characteristic of Judaism. The *principle* of the system is one thing; the *form* is quite another. What, then, is the principle, as distinguished from the form, of the thing? It is this: The idea that our position in eternity is *conditioned* upon external relations and circumstances, and not upon moral character exclusively, upon anything other than real holiness or heart purity. The Jew rested his hope of salvation wholly upon circumstances external to the state of his heart. This was the *principle* of his system. Nor can we now fail to perceive that a system of religion may be wholly Judaistic in principle, though totally diverse in form from Judaism itself. That system, whatever its form or by whatever name it may be called, is really and radically Judaistic, and is only another form of the same thing, which conditionates salvation upon anything whatever, other than true holiness of heart.

V. Some of the particular forms of modern Judaism next claim our attention. Among these, I notice the following, as deserving special attention:—

1. Placing the condition of salvation in our connection with, or a standing in some particular sect or denomination, instead of conditioning our destiny exclusively on what the Bible does, "repentance towards God, and faith toward our Lord Jesus Christ." Of this, Romanism is an example. In all such systems, a community so called Christian has been substituted for the Jewish, and connection with that community for descent from Abraham. Only a different form of the same thing, to wit, external relations, has been substituted for "God's righteousness."

2. Another form of modern Judaism consists in placing the conditions of salvation on subjection to particular *ordinances*, such as Baptism or the Lord's Supper, ordinances duly administered. When the fact of our becoming regenerated, and "receiving power to become the sons of God," is made to turn, not upon our receiving Christ directly and immediately by faith, but upon our being subject to the ordinance of baptism, what is this but another form of Judaism baptized with the name of Christian? The remains of two infants, who died at the same age, are before us; one was subjected to the ordinance of baptism, and the other not. What must we think of a system of religion, calling itself Christ, that would affirm, that for such a reason the soul of one of these is now in the kingdom of darkness? If all who die in infancy are saved, then baptism, as far as regeneration and translation into the kingdom of grace is concerned, is of no real use. The soul is just as well off without it as with it; and it is the height of

absurdity to talk about an individual's being regenerated and made an heir of the kingdom of God "by baptism." If all infants, who die unbaptized, are lost, and lost for the reason that they were not baptized, then the immortal destiny of nearly half the race is made to turn wholly upon mere accidental external relations, in respect to the existence of which neither the saved or lost had any knowledge, choice, nor agency. What is such a system, but one of the grossest and most irrational and unchristian forms of Chistianized Judaism of which humanity, in its darkest speculations, ever conceived? Suppose a child is taken into the house of God, and there receives the ordinance of baptism, with an avowed atheist for a godfather, (the very circumstances in which a particular friend of mine received the ordinance,) what infinite credulity must posses a mind that, witnessing no change whatever in the subsequent dispositions or manifestations of the child, can then see it grow, as in fact often the case, directly up, as it advances in age, into a giant in depravity, and with no form of virtue attaching to it, and yet believe that that child was really and truly regenerated, and made an heir of the kingdom of God, in and by that ordinance! Two children, we will further suppose, are before us, presenting, in all respects, the same or similar manifestations; one has received the ordinance of baptism, and the other has not. Yet we are to believe, in the presence of the same fruits, that one of these children is a truly spiritual regenerated person, and an heir of life eternal, and the other a child of wrath! But suppose, once more, that the individual who has received the ordinance grows up visibly a monster in depravity; while the other, without ever having received the ordinance, in the so-called apostolic form, and having never been convinced of the necessity of receiving it, or even suspected it, yet, according to the best light given him, he has "served God with a pure conscience." In the presence of such fruits, we are to regard the former as having been "spiritually regenerated," and the other as "having no hope, and being without God in the world." Thus we are required to reverse wholly the Savior's rule, and say, "By their fruits ye shall *not* know them," but ye shall know them by mere external relations, which imply in themselves no form or degree of holiness whatever, nor the most distant approach to any proper manifestations of it. All this we are expected to believe, in the presence of the most undeniable fact that the Bible never gives the shadow of an intimation, near or remote, that regeneration is by baptism; and when God himself has given us a formal definition of the "baptism that does save us,"—a baptism which consists not in "the putting away of the filth of the flesh," that is, does not consist in any outward ordinances, "but in the answer of a good conscience towards God," that is, "in righteousness and holiness." What an infinite mistake the Holy Ghost made, in "sending Paul not to baptize, but to preach the Gospel," if spiritual regeneration is, not "by the foolishness of preaching," but "by baptism!"

3. The third form of Christianized Judaism demanding attention, consists in practically conditionating salvation upon the relations of the intelligence to certain systems of doctrine, rather than in practical godliness. The relations of the intellect to the truth are as distinct from the state of the heart, as external ordinances. Holiness of heart is no more implied in, or necessarily connected with, mere intellectually assent to any system of doctrine, than regeneration is with baptism. Simon Magus was baptized, and yet remained in the "gall of bitterness and bonds of iniquity." So a man may "understand all mysteries and all knowledge," and yet be "as sounding brass and a tinkling cymbal." Now, where a main's standing in a church depends rather upon imputed soundness in doctrine than upon a holy life, where a church can "bear those that are evil," but cannot endure in her members dissent from her creed, on points acknowledged to be not essential to real holiness, we have in all such cases Judaism in principle, as really and truly as in either of the cases above named.

4. The last form of this error that I notice conditionates salvation not upon *present* obedience, but upon the relations of the individual to some supposed change of character in

some *past time*. Salvation, in this case, is made to turn upon what is as really and truly external to the *now* state of the heart, as in any system of formalism that ever existed. That form of the doctrine of saints' perseverance which affirms that "we are partakers of Christ," not "if we hold the beginning of our confidence steadfast unto the end," but if we have been once regenerated, is nothing but Judaism under a Christian name.

LECTURE V.

ELECTION.

2 PETER i. 10.
"Wherefore the rather, brethren, give diligence to make your calling and election sure; for if you do these things, ye shall never fail."

THERE are three words, of not unfrequent use, in the New Testament, which are quite commonly supposed to be employed to designate the doctrine of eternal and unconditional election, to wit, the noun rendered "election,"—the adjective rendered "elect,"—and the original verb from which each of these is derived, the verb generally rendered "chosen." The verb is used just twenty times, the adjective twenty-three times, and the noun seven times, in the New Testament. To understand the bearing of these words upon the doctrine under consideration, we must, in the first place, determine the nature of the doctrine itself. The doctrine of election, as everywhere held by its advocates, is this: God, foreseeing from eternity all mankind in a state of sin and ruin; and while no reasons whatever, as far as character of men is concerned, presented themselves to the divine mind why one should be selected as an heir of life rather than another, and when it was not just as practicable for him to save one as another, and all as a part, had he seen it wise and best so to do, determined, from eternity, to select out of the mass a certain fixed and definite number of individuals as heirs of everlasting life—a number which, by no possibility, can be either increased or diminished. Upon this fixed and definite number God determined from eternity to bring to bear a divine influence, in the time and under the circumstances unchangeably fixed and pre-determined,—an influence which would infallibly secure in them a fitness for eternal life. The remaining portion of mankind, God, in his sovereignty, eternally determined to pass over, and leave to perish in their sins. The former class are called the elect, and the later, the reprobate. God's plan, in respect to these two classes, is denominated the doctrines of eternal and unconditional election and reprobation. Election to life is said to be unconditional, because it rests upon no conditions foreseen as complied with on the part of the elect. Such is the doctrine of election. A part only are elected, when the whole might have been just as well, and God seen it wise so to do. This part are elected without any reasons whatever forseen in them why they should be saved rather than others. Everything rests wholly upon the sovereign election of God. It has been my honest aim not to pervert the views of my brethren holding this doctrine, but to present such views as they themselves actually hold them. It is according to the views above defined that they suppose the words elect, election, and chosen, are used in the New Testament. The question for us, as students of the Bible and pupils of the Holy Spirit to determine, is this: Is this the idea which we ought to attach to these terms when we meet with them in the Scriptures? As preparatory to a direct consideration of the various passages in which these words are found, I would invite very special attention to the following preliminary observations.

1. It is obviously contrary to all our natural ideas of a Being of perfect wisdom and goodness, that he would make such a difference between moral agents, as the doctrines of election and reprobation suppose, without there being reasons all-sufficient, intrinsic in the character of such agents themselves, for such momentous discriminations between them. When a Being of perfect wisdom and rectitude elects one object for one purpose, we naturally suppose that such selections are based upon reasons perceived as intrinsic in the objects,—reasons demanding the diverse uses to which they are respectfully assigned. All our ideas of fitness are shocked at the mere *suggestion* that such a wide discrimination has not its basis in a corresponding difference, intrinsic in the character of the objects on which the acts referred to terminate. No such acts, we cannot but judge, ought to be based upon the mere will or sovereign pleasure of any being. All acts of will,

on the other hand, (is it irreverential in a creature to say?) ought to be in harmony with intelligence, to be demanded by the dictates of perfect wisdom, and to be put forth for the reason alone that they are thus demanded. Now, when we contemplate the Most High as bringing two moral agents into being, agents divinely endowed with capacities for endless progress in knowledge, and consequent capacities for virtue or vice, and happiness or misery, it is certainly contrary to all our ideas of what is fit and proper in a Being thus related to such agents,—a Being of infinite wisdom and rectitude,—to suppose that he has selected one of them as an heir of life eternal, and the other as a victim of eternal pain and suffering, without there being reasons of infinite weight, reasons intrinsic in their characters, for such a separation.

2. When God makes eternal separation between them, he always assigns reasons intrinsic in their characters as the sole grounds for that separation. "Come, ye blessed of my Father—*for* I was hungered and you gave me meat." "Depart, ye cursed—*for* I was an hungered, and ye gave me no meat." The term *for*, in these several instances, expresses the reasons for the election and reprobation of the diverse classes of moral agents before us, the reasons in view of which God vindicates his own adjudications before the universe. The entire representations of Scriptrue, on this important subject, are in perfect harmony with these declarations of Christ: "Who will render to every man according to his deeds."—"All that are in their graves shall hear his voice, and shall come forth; they that have done good unto the resurrection of life, and they that have done evil unto the resurrection of damnation."

Since such is the basis of all the procedures of the judgment in which the final discrimination between mankind is to be made, if God has any predeterminations or purposes of election, in respect to such discriminations, may we not safely conclude that they have their basis wholly on the grounds foreseen by him, on which the discrimination is made, that is, "the deeds," in view of which, and for the avowed reasons which, the awards of the great day are dispensed? If this be the character of the electing grace and reprobating judgment of God, then we have an election and reprobation which must, when understood, "commend themselves to every man's conscience in the sight of God."

But how does this great transaction appear when contemplated in the light of the doctrine under consideration? According to this doctrine, all events alike are eternally predetermined by God. Its fundamental teachings are, that "God hath, for his own glory, *unchangeably* foreordained *whatsoever* comes to pass." The fall of man, then, and all our states and acts, as sinners, as these are events which do come to pass, must as really and truly be the objects of an unchangeable decree, as the salvation and holiness of the righteous. Whatever is not thus predetermined, the advocates of this doctrine affirm, is left to chance; and as nothing, as they affirm, is thus left, all things alike must, of course, be fixed, and inevitably so, by an eternal decree. If any who maintain the doctrine of decrees deny any of these statements, they must deny the fundamental article of their system; to wit, that "God has unchangeably foreordained whatsoever comes to pass." They must, according to their own principles, affirm that the occurrence of some events is left to chance.

Suppose, now, that when the finally reprobate are about to receive that doom, the fact stands revealed that the character and acts for which they are to receive that doom were all unchangeably rendered what they were by an eternal, all-necessitating decree of God, and consequently that the exclusive *final* cause of their doom is, not their own voluntary choice of evil instead of good, but God's own purpose necessarily rendering that choice what it was. When the principles of that transaction are thus unveiled before the intelligence of the universe, how will appear? Could God's judgments, thus contemplated, appear "true and righteous altogether?" I conclude, then, that when God assigns the moral character of men as the sole cause of the discrimination there to be made between the saints and sinners, he assigns the true and real grounds of all his own predeterminations pertaining to their election on the one hand, or their reprobation on the other. God's preëlecting grace, and pre-reprobationg judgments, must have their basis exclusively in the foreseen free, voluntary acts of men, in accepting or rejecting offered mercy. Against all such elections no conceivable objections can be brought. God's simple foreknowledge of what men, in the exercise of their uninterrupted free agency, will do, in no sense or degree determines their acts one way or the other. Men, under the influence which God brings to bear upon them for their own eternal good, determine their own character as sinful or holy. Whatever purposes God has formed in respect to men,—purposes resting wholly upon their character foreseen,—no reasonable mind can object against. Such a form of election as this cannot be unworthy of God, as the moral governor of the universe.

3. I will now notice an idea fundamentally false, as it appears to me, professedly based upon the great truth that God is our Creator. Because he sustains this relation to us, he has a right, it is said, to dispose of us as his property, according to his own sovereign pleasure,—to appoint one to life, and others directly or indirectly to death, as may be his will. Now, to me it is a truth self-evident, that the highest conceivable reasons why God should not, without consideration of infinite and eternal weight, destroy the happiness of such a creature, are involved in the great fact that he, by his own voluntary act, has brought that creature into being, and has endowed him with all his capacities for good or evil. What is one of the main reasons for parental obligation to care for the necessities of children? The very fact that the parent, by his own voluntary act, has been the cause of the existence of the child. Such reasons must apply with equal weight to God, as the Infinite Father of the great family of the rational universe. God certainly, without reasons of eternal weight, does not claim the right to cut off a creature from the infinite good to which he has himself adapted the nature of that creature. The contrary idea has its origin exclusively in the pro-slavery

conception of property in man. Man is not a thing, and neither does God claim, nor can man rightly claim, property in him. As a moral agent, he stands eternally excluded from the idea of property. He can forfeit his right to good only by crime, and crime can exist only as the exclusive result of the voluntary act of a free moral agent.

We are now prepared for a direct consideration of the meaning of the terms elect, election, and chosen, as they are applied to men in the New Testament. The question is, Do they represent an election which has no basis whatever in the intrinsic character of the objects, character making a difference wide and fundamental between them and the non-elect, and therefore demanding that this difference shall be made between them? Or is it, what all wise and just elections of this character, in all other instances, are, an election in which a wise and just discrimination is made where, and only where, such a discrimination is demanded by what is intrinsic in the character of the objects of such election?

If we refer to the primary significations of the words under consideration, there can be no doubt whatever as to the meaning which we should attach to them. They always, according to their primary signification, designate an election in which one object is preferred to another, on the exclusive ground of the perceived or imputed superior excellence of the former over the later. Thus the primary signification of the word elect, according to the distinguished lexicographer, Professor Robinson, is, "*select, choice, excellent.*" According to this definition, the term elect can be applied to an object when, and only when, it possesses superior intrinsic excellence which requires that it should be preferred to other of the same class. The question is, Is this the meaning of the term when applied to men in the Scriptures? Are they God's elect, if the are such, because they are the objects of his moral approbation and favor, on account of the beauty of holiness which he sees in *them*, and not in others?

[A word of explanation is demanded here. When I speak of reasons, instrinsic in the character of men, why one should be saved and the other lost, I would, by no means, be understood as supposing that salvation is not, from first to last, wholly by grace, and more than we are to suppose the Bible to teach this doctrine, because it asserts that men shall be "judged according to their works." Salvation is all of grace; yet it is proffered on certain irreversible conditions. Those intrinsic in their character why they should or should not become "heirs of the grace of life." Such reasons do not imply that those who are saved receive eternal life on the ground of merit in themselves, and not wholly as a gift of grace.]

That we may come to a right understanding of this subject, we will first consider the meaning of these terms when applied to our Saviour. "To whom (Christ) coming, as unto a living stone, disallowed indeed of men, but chosen (elect) of God and precious." I Pet. ii. 4. "Wherefore it is contained in the Scripture, Behold, I lay in Sion a chief cornerstone, elect, precious; and he that believeth on him shall not be confounded." I Pet. ii. 6. "Let him save himself if he be the Christ, the chosen (elect) of God." Luke xxiii. 35. The original word rendered *chosen* and *elect* in these passages is, in all instances, one and the same. So it will be the case in all the passages which I shall hereafter select. The only difference that ever occurs is, that in two or three instances the participle instead of the adjective is used. There is no difference of meaning, however, in any instance. Now, of the meaning of the term *elect*, when applied to Christ, there can, by no possibility, be any doubt. It never can designate an object in itself not to be preferred to others, but which, by an act of sovereignty, has been selected out from a class in themselves all equally eligible, and then rendered precious, by an influence subsequently brought to bear upon it. It designates, on the other hand, precisely the opposite idea, that of an object in itself preferable to others, and, for that reason, selected out from among them. The figure employed is that of a builder seeking a rock in itself adapted to occupy the place of the chief corner-stone on which the entire building is to be founded, and having found one, of all others to be preferred for this end, selects it accordingly. Hence it is called "elect, precious." Such was the meaning of the term when applied to Christ, by his enemies, "If he be Christ, the chosen (elect) of God," that is, if he is, as he professed to be, so dear to God, on account of his transcendent excellence.

We find the same terms applied to men, also, in connections which render their meaning equally manifest. "Then pleased it the apostles and elders, with the whole church, to send chosen men of their own company to Antioch with Paul and Barnabas: *namely*, Judas surnamed Barabas, and Silas, chief men among the brethren." "It seemed good unto us, being assembled with one accord, to send chosen men unto you with our beloved Barnabas and Paul." The term chosen, in both the above passages, can have but one meaning. It implies, in the individuals elected, superior qualifications for the mission on which they were sent. For this reason, they are called "chosen men." Thus we are accustomed to call individuals of superior excellence "choice spirits." You will now understand clearly the meaning of the same term when applied to Paul, (Acts ix. 15.) "He is a chosen vessel (literally vessel of election) unto me, to bear my name before the Gentiles." The evident meaning is, he is a very precious vessel unto me; a vessel, on account of his present character and superior qualifications, worthy to be selected from among all others for the high office of "bearing my name before the Gentiles." There is nothing in the term, as here used, that, in the most distant form, even looks towards an eternal, unconditional election, whom there is no reason in the object why it should be selected rather than others of the same class. God only speaks of Paul in view of what he then was, as a truly converted man.

Equally manifest is the meaning of the term applied to Christians generally and indiscriminately, (1 Peter ii. 9.) "But ye are a chosen (elect) generation, a royal priesthood, a holy nation, a peculiar people." The meaning of the term, as applied to Christ, in the verse preceding, we have already understood. In the same sense, all the laws of language compel us to understand it in the verse before us. Such are the connections in which it is here found, that no honest mind can mistake its meaning. An elect generation is one which, on account of its superior and royal moral excellence, is worthy to be selected from the rest of mankind, as the objects of divine approbation and favor.

No less plain is the meaning of the term in Rev. xvii. 14. "For he (Christ) is Lord of lords, and King of kings, and they that are with him are called and chosen (elect) and faithful;" that is, Christ himself is superior to all others, and his glorified associates are, on account of their transcendent excellence, worthy to be his companions and associates. The connection in which the term "elect" is her found, renders that this must be its meaning in this passage.

The term "called," here found, and which is often applied to the saints in the Scriptures of the New Testament, demands a special explanation, in this connection. The term is figurative, and is taken from the customs which obtained in the ancient regal feasts. When a monarch would make a feast, he was accustomed, as we learn, (Matt. xxii. 1—3, and elsewhere,) to send out first and notify individuals, that at the time appointed they would be invited to the royal feast that was to be celebrated. The notice and the final invitation were denominated the calling to the feast. As the guest were selected on account of their high standing, and for their superior worth in the monarch's estimation, to receive such a call was a mark of great distinction. Hence the guests, as expressive of such distinction, were denominated the *called* ones, the called of the king; that is, individuals standing high in royal estimation. This is the great and exclusive idea to be attached to the term when applied to saints, in the passage above cited from Revelation, and in all other passages where they are denominated "the called of God," "called saints," not "called to be saints," as rendered in our translation. In all instances in which we read "called to be saints," "called to be an apostle," &c., the literal rendering is "called saints," and "called apostle." The adjective *called*, when thus applied, never,—I am quite safe in the affirmation,—in any single instance, designates what is denominated "effectually calling." It is always employed as a term of distinction, to designate those who are, on account of their superior excellence, dear to God, and consequently invited by him to the "marriage supper of the Lamb," or to the enjoyment of high and distinguished privileges.

We are now prepared to explain the passage in 2 Peter i. 10, in which both the terms "calling" and "election" are found. "Wherefore the rather, brethren, give diligence to make your calling and election sure; for if ye do these things, ye shall never fall." The election and calling, here referred to, are undeniably future; because they are yet uncertain and conditioned on the voluntary conduct of the creature. Reference is had to the time when "God is to make up his jewels," and when he is to invite all who are his to the great feast of heaven. The meaning of the passage is, Give all diligence to live so as to render it certain that when that period shall arrive, you will be among the called and elected of God. No construction conceivable can be more forced, unnatural, and opposite to all the laws of language, than the high Calvinistic explanation, which makes the passage mean this—make it certain to yourselves that you were from all eternity called and elected of God. Calling, to say the least, must be in time, and not from eternity; and as this is and must be future, so must the election here referred to be future.

The meaning of 1 Peter ii. 2, now becomes obvious:— "Elect, according to the foreknowledge of God the Father, through sanctification of the Spirit, unto obedience and sprinkling of the blood of Jesus Christ; grace unto you, and peace be multiplied." Three important truths are taught in this passage. 1. That Christians are sanctified and saved through the influence of the Spirit and grace of Christ. That they are not passive but active recipients of this divine influence, and that as such recipients of this divine influence, and that as such recipients they may properly be said to purify themselves by yielding of their own free will to this influence, we learn from the 22d verse of this same chapter:—"Ye have purified yourselves by obeying the truth, through the Spirit,"—that is, ye have rendered yourselves pure, by yielding, of your own choice, to the truth, presented to your minds by the Spirit. 2. The second great truth that we have from this passage is this:—Believers became the elect of God in consequence of having thus obeyed the truth through the Spirit. 3. All these are divinely foreseen results of God's gracious arrangement for the redemption of men. By no stretch of language can anything in this passage be made to bear in favor of the doctrine of eternal, unconditional election. An election foreseen as actually taking place in time, and in consequence of terms of life being complied with, is a very different form of doctrine from that above stated. Rom. ii. 5: "Even so, then, at this present time, also, there is a remnant according to the election of grace,"—that is, the kind, gracious, benignant election of God, as opposed to the ungracious and arbitrary arrangement. According to this election, there was, as Paul affirms, a remnant among the Jews who were numbered among the elect of God.

1 Thess. i. 4: "Knowing, brethren, beloved, your election of God," that is, calling to remembrance the circumstances in which you, in the midst of the fiercest contentions, and most embittered persecutions, as the apostle shows in the verse following, embraced the gospel, and thus became beloved elected once of God. As the election here referred to place in time, no reference can be had in the passage to the doctrine of eternal, unconditional election.

As Rom. ix. 11, "That the purpose of God according to election might stand," has been explained in a former lecture, nothing in addition is demanded in respect tot he passage in this connection. The election here referred to pertained exclusively to nations, as such, and not to individuals, and had no reference whatever to an election to eternal life.

A mere passing remark is all that is now required in explaining the phrase, "Many are called, but few chosen," found in Matt. xx. 16; xxii. 14. All that this phrase can be made to mean is this: Many, that is, all, are invited to partake of the salvation of God; but few, however, in consequence of accepting the offer, are elected as heirs of life eternal. I suppose that a still different construction should be put upon this phrase; but as it has no particular bearing upon our present inquiries, I pass it over.

As the terms *elect* and *election* imply something valuable and excellent in the object, something on account of which it is selected in preference to others of the same class, they are hence sometimes used in the Scriptures as terms of very tender endearment; as, for example, "the elect lady," and the "elect sister,"—that is, the precious beloved Christian lady and sister; 2 John 1 and 13. "Shall not God avenge (answer the prayers) of his own elect?" Luke xvii. 7. His own elect,—that is, those who, on account of their character, are dear and precious in God's sight, and, as such, have been chosen by him out of the world. "Who shall lay anything to the charge of God's elect?" Rom. viii. 33; that is, who will appear in judgment against those whom, on account of their character, God has selected as dear and precious before him? "And shall gather together his elect," (his own precious chosen ones.) Matt. xxiv. 31; Mark xiii. 27. "For the elect's sake whom he hath chosen," (his own precious elected ones.) Matt. xxiv. 22; Mark xiii. 20. "Salute Rufus, chosen in the Lord,"—that is, an honored, precious, beloved disciple of Christ. Rom. xvi. 13. "Put on, therefore, as the elect of God," (holy and beloved,)—that is, as the holy and beloved chosen ones of God,—"bowels of mercies, kindness," &c. Col. iii. 12. "According to the faith of God's elect," (God's chosen ones.) Tit. i. 1.

As believers only are thus elected by God, these terms are often used in the Scriptures as synonymous with the term *Christian* or *believer,* always including the idea of preciousness on account of character. In this sense they are to be explained in such passages as the following:—2 Tim. ii. 10: "All things are for the elect's sake,"—for the good of believers. Matt. xiii. 24: "To deceive, if it were possible, the very elect." Rom. xi. 7: "Bu the election (believers) hath obtained it, (the salvation of Christ,) and the rest (Jews and unbelievers) were blinded." Rom. xi. 28: "As concerning the gospel, they are enemies for your sake; but as touching the election, they are beloved for the Father's sake." The meaning of this passage, as I suppose, may be thus expressed. As far as the gospel is concerned, they, the mass of the Jews, are its embittered enemies, because you Gentiles are introduced into the fold of Christ; but as far as the "election" is concerned, the remnant of true believers among them, these are very dear to God, not only on account of their character as believers, but as the decedents of the ancient patriarchs. Whether this is the true explanation or not, the passage cannot be explained so as to have any bearing in favor of the doctrine of eternal and unconditional election. There is one passage (1 Tim. iv. 21) in which the term elect is applied to angels. "I charge thee before God, and the Lord Jesus Christ, and the elect angels." Here the term evidently has the meaning of holy, beloved of God, and therefore to be held in esteem by us. The meaning of the passage is: I charge thee before God, and the Lord Jesus Christ, and the high principalities of heaven.

I have thus completed my promise, as far as the passages in which the terms elect and election, found in the New Testament, are concerned. I have, I believe, omitted not a single passage in which either of these terms, or the original word which they represent, appears. You now have a distinct exposition of the meaning which, as I suppose, should be attached to them, and are able, if the explanation given is admitted as the correct one, to judge for yourselves in respect to their bearings upon the doctrine of eternal and unconditional election. It now remains to consider several other passages in which these terms do not appear, but which are supposed to sustain, either directly or indirectly, this doctrine.

1. There is one class of passages which is supposed to teach this doctrine not directly, but by manifest implication; those passages especially which are deemed to affirm the fact of the sinner's total inability to anything that is good. If the sinner lacks all ability to do what is right, then his salvation must depend wholly upon a sovereign act of God, an act conditioned of course upon a purpose of eternal and unconditional election.

The first passage that I notice, which is supposed to affirm this doctrine, is found in Jer. xiii. 23: "Can the Ethiopian change his skin?" &c. This is adduced as affirming the absolute inability of *all* sinners to "cease to do evil, and learn to do well." In reply, I remark, 1. This passage, instead of being applicable to *all* sinners, is most undeniably applicable only to a part; those "who are *accustomed* to do evil."—that is, those who have become confirmed in the *habit* of sinning. 2. The inability affirmed of this particular class, whatever the nature of such impotency may be, is one which wholly results from long-continuance in sin, and consists exclusively in the power or tendency of habit thus acquired. 3. The form of inability, therefore, is to be totally denied of the mass of sinners, that is, of all those who have not become confirmed in the habit of sin. 4. This passage, then, when rightly understood, teaches, most plainly and undeniably, the very doctrine which it is supposed to deny, to whit, the ability of the sinner to do what is good. If men have not the power to do right or wrong, they can never generate in themselves a tendency to do, or confirm themselves in the habit of doing, the one in distinction from the other. If all mankind are alike in the state of total incapacity to do anything but sin, then it is the height of absurdity to speak of their disabling themselves from ceasing to sin, by being accustomed to sin. 5. Nothing is or can be further from the design of inspiration, in this passage, than to affirm that an absolute incapacity to holiness is acquired even by the habit of sinning. The simple truth here taught is this: the sinner, by accustoming himself to sin, becomes at length so confirmed in the habit of sinning, that his reformation becomes hopeless. It is a most fatal perversion of the passage to make any other use of it than as a warning against "accustoming ourselves to do evil."

The passage which next claims our attention is John vi. 43. "No many can come to me, except the Father which hath sent me draw him; and I will raise him up at the last day." To be "drawn" to Christ, in the sense of this passage, is, as we learn from the next verse, to be "taught of God." The doctrine announced is, that no man can attain to a saving knowledge of Christ unless he is taught of God. That which cuts the sinner off from the divine teaching under consideration, renders it impracticable from him to come to Christ. To indulge a cavilling spirit, instead of opening the heart to divine teaching, accomplishes this fearful result. To warn his enemies against the indulgence of such a spirit, and thus to prevent their cutting themselves off from divine teaching, is the exclusive object of Christ, in this passage. The Jews had been cavilling at our Saviour's word. "Murmur not among yourselves," he says,—that is, I beseech you not to indulge this cavilling spirit. You will thereby wholly cut yourselves off from the divine teaching or drawing, without which no man can come to me. It is fully implied in our Saviour's words, that the sinner is able to avail himself of divine teaching, and he is simply warned against that act of suicide, by which, in the indulgence of a cavilling spirit, he would cut himself off from this infinite good. To draw the conclusion from this passage that the sinner cannot cease his cavils and avail himself of divine teaching so as to come to Christ, is to do that which has but one tendency, and that a most fatal one, to feat the every end which Christ had in view in the utterance of this truth. His exclusive design was to present the strongest possible motive for the suppression in ourselves of the captious, cavilling spirit against the truth. To draw from such an announcement the doctrine of the total impotency of the sinner to all good,—in other words, to tell him, when cavilling against the truth, that he cannot cease doing it, and yield himself to divine teaching,—is to reverse wholly our Saviour's benevolent intentions in all he said on that occasion. One other passage demands attention in this connection. Rom. viii. 8: "So then they that are in the flesh cannot please God." The doctrine here taught is so plain, that it is a matter of no little surprise that any should have misapprehended it. Paul is offering reasons why we should cease to live after the flesh, and, by the mortification of the deeds of the body, become heirs of eternal life. He has not certainly been guilty of the strange folly of urging us to do this by the presentation of the consideration that it is impossible for us to do it. The real idea presented by the apostle is this. Our salvation depends upon our pleasing God. Living after the flesh is wholly incompatible with doing this. Pleasing God and minding the things of the flesh cannot coëxist in the heart. Therefore we should cease living after the flesh.

2. In still another class of passages conversion is ascribed to God, in such a form and manner, as clearly to affirm the doctrine of eternal and unconditional election. Of this class, Ps. cx. 3 is often quoted: "Thy people *shall be* willing in the day of thy power, in the beauties of holiness from the womb of the morning: thou hast the dew of thy youth." The explanation which some give of the first clause is this:—Sinners shall be converted at the time when God, by his own omnipotence, changes their nature, or constrains them to repent; and that in conformity to his own eternal and unconditional purpose of election. This construction is based upon a total misunderstanding of the whole passage, (it being utterly impossible to attach any meaning whatever to the most of it,) and consequently not perceiving the real connection of the first clause what immediately follows. The true meaning of the passage, according to the original Hebrew, may be thus expressed:—Thy people (those already converted) shall be volunteers (literally voluntariness) in the day of thy glorious war, in holy garments, (or clad in the beauty of holiness.) More than the dew-drops from the womb of the morning shall be thy youth; the youth who shall

arrange themselves under thy banners. Christ is presented to our contemplation under the figure of a glorious conqueror marching forth at the head of the sacramental host, for the spiritual conquest of the world. His people, that is, those who are then his real followers, are to volunteer their services with the intensest ardor. So numerous are his self-consecrated host then to be, that even the young men about his standard will be more numerous than the dew-drops from the womb of the morning. The passage, then, simply and exclusively relates to the spirit with which the Church, in the progress of her future history, will be imbued, relatively to the salvation of the world, and has no relation whatever to the doctrine which it is adduced to prove, the nature of the divine influence in the conversion of sinners.

To the same purpose Eph. ii. 1 is often cited:—"And you hath he quickened, who were dead in trespasses and sins." From the fact that sinners are here said to be "dead in (on account of) trespasses and sins," it is inferred, that they are totally disabled to all good, and can be rendered holy only by an act of divine sovereignty in conformity to an eternal decree of election. Now, if we are to infer the sinner's absolute inability to holiness, because he is said to be dead *in* sin, we should conclude that it is impossible for any real Christian ever to sin again; for they are positively declared to be dead *to* sin. "Ye are dead." Two important truths are plainly taught in this passage. 1. Sinners are dead, under condemnation to death, on account of their sins. 2. They are recovered from this state by the spirit and grace of Christ. But whether they are active or passive under this divine influence, nothing whatever is here affirmed one way or the other. On this important point full and distinct information is imparted to us in other portions of the divine word. Sinners, as we there learn, pass from death unto life, by receiving by faith the truth presented to their minds by the Spirit. "Ye have purified yourselves by obeying the truth through the Spirit." The Spirit quickens the sinner by presenting the truth to his mind. The sinner purifies himself by obeying the truth, or voluntarily yielding to the truth thus presented to his election. The quickening is one in which divine and human activity voluntarily combine and harmonize. Any idea of conversion or regeneration which would separate these two agencies in the change, "puts asunder what God has joined together,"—a fatal divorcement not unfrequently resulting from the folly of human speculation.

3. There is one other class of passages which are supposed, by some, to have a fundamental bearing in favor of the doctrine under consideration,—passages in which it is affirmed to be directly and immediately taught. Of these, Rom. viii, 29, 30, is reckoned as one of the most important:—"For whom he did foreknow, he also did predestinate *to be* conformed to the image of his Son, that he might be the first-born among many brethren. Moreover, whom he did predestinate, them he also called; and whom he called, them he also justified; and whom he justified, them he also glorified." In the preceding part of the chapter, the apostle assures us, that "if we live after the flesh, we shall die; but if we through the Spirit do mortify the deeds of the body, we shall live." In the verse preceding the one above cited, we are told, as a reason for obeying such truths, of the blessedness of all who obey and love God: "And we know that all things work together for good to them that love God, to them who are the called according to *his* purpose." The calling here referred to takes place in time, and is not at all from eternity. This we learn from verse 30. To be "called according to God's purpose," means to be invited to a participation of eternal life, in conformity to a preärrangement of divine grace. This all will admit. The object of the apostle, in verses 29, 30, is to give the reasons why "all things shall work together for good to them that love God." This is evident from the particle "for," with which these verses are introduced! What a strange reason this would be to assign for the proof of such a fact, to wit, that all who have from all eternity been unconditionally elected will be saved! If you will not "live after the flesh, but through the Spirit will mortify the deeds of the body," and

continue to love God, "all things shall work together for your good." What is the evidence of this fact? Why, this. All who were from all eternity unconditionally elected shall be saved. Where is the connection between two such propositions as these? Paul certainly was never guilty of reasoning thus illogically. What, then, is the real meaning? After saying that "all things work together for good to them that love God," he proceeds to present the reasons for the assurance of such a result in the experience of all such. The reasons are the following:—1. All whom God foresaw would exercise this love, he predetermined, in consequence of foreseeing this virtue in them, to perfect their character into a perfect likeness to the image of Christ. So he is represented, in the fulfilment of this purpose, as giving them his Spirit, that they, "with an open face beholding as in a glass the glory of the Lord, may be changed into the same image from glory to glory, even as by the Spirit of the Lord." 2. "All whom he thus predestinates, he also calls," (invites to a participation of life eternal.) 3. "All whom he calls he also justifies," (fully pardons all their iniquities,) and all "whom he thus pardons he glorifies" in heaven at last. Such is God's fixed arrangement in respect to all whom he foresees as loving him. We have only "to keep ourselves in the love of God," and we shall become, with infallible certainty, the objects of this divine arrangement. What a motive thus to keep ourselves! We must bear in mind that the predestination referred to in the passage is based wholly and exclusively upon God's foreknowledge of what creatures, in a voluntary compliance with the influence of his own Spirit, will become. "Whom he did foreknow." Foreknow as what? As actually loving him. This is the exclusive subject of the apostle's remarks. "All things work together for good to them that love God." Why? Because that all whom God did foreknow as doing this, "he did predestinate." There is nothing whatever in the passage which has the most distant reference to an eternal unconditional election among sinners who do not love God at all, electing some of these to salvation, and leaving the rest to perish in their sins. To put this construction upon it annihilates wholly its power to accomplish the purpose for which alone it was written, namely, to present an all-constraining motive for "keeping ourselves in the love of God."

Eph. i. 4, 5, is another passage most confidently relied upon to sustain this doctrine. "According as he hath chosen us in him before the foundation of the world, that we should be holy and without blame before him in love. Having predestined us unto the adoption of children by Jesus Christ to himself, according to the good pleasure of his will." The phrase, "chosen us in him," admits of two constructions; to wit, chosen us *to be* in him, or chosen us who *are* in him. There can be no reasonable doubt that the latter is the true meaning. Were the former one the correct explanation, the words "to be," which, in the original, appear before the words "holy and without blame," would stand before the phrase "in him." The meaning of the passage, then, is this. According as he hath chosen us, who are in Christ, that is, true believers, and chosen us to be, or chosen that we should be, "holy and without blame before him in love." Having predestinated us unto the adoption of children, or predetermined to adopt us as children, &c. Now for God, before the foundation of the world, to choose that all who truly believe in Christ should be without blame before him in love, and for him to predetermine the adoption of all such as his children, is one thing; for him, form all eternity, to elect, unconditionally, a certain portion of sinners to life eternal, and to determinate to leave the remainder to perish in their sins, when he might just as well have saved one part as the another, and the whole as a part, had he seen it best so to do, is quite another thing. With this latter doctrine the passage under consideration has no connection whatever, unless it be that of opposition. The exclusive object of the apostle is to reveal to Christians God's purposes and arrangements of holy love, grace and mercy towards them, *as believers in Christ*, and because of their relation to him as sinners saved by grace through him. No greater perversion can possibly be made of the passage than to use it in support of the doctrine of eternal and unconditional election and reprobation.

The meaning of verse 11, of this same chapter, now becomes plain:—"In whom also we have obtained an inheritance, being predestinated according to the purpose of him who worketh all things after the counsel of his own will." The predestination here referred to is a predestination of *believers*, as such, to the inheritance of life eternal, and that, in consequence of their foreseen acceptance of mercy. Nothing is said, or intimated, of a predesitination of a portion of sinners to conversion, and consequent salvation, while the rest, in the fulfilment of an eternal decree, are left to perish in sin. The "working of all things after the counsel of his own will," refers to the certainty of God's carrying into accomplishment all his predetermined arrangements in respect to believers. It is very singular that high Calvinists cite this passage in proof of a proposition strictly universal, to wit, that God brings to pass all events according to his eternal decrees, and that they then deny what is necessarily implied in their own construction; to wit, that God is the efficient cause of sin.

Acts xiii. 48: "And as many as were ordained to eternal life believed." The original word here rendered "ordained" is a military term, and refers to an army's taking rank, or voluntarily arranging themselves, in obedience to the order of their commander. The apostle is represented, in the context, as giving the word of command to sinners, to arrange themselves for eternal life, by believing in Christ. We are here told, that as many as in obedience to that order were voluntarily arranged for eternal life, believed in Christ. This, I have not doubt, from the laws of language, is, and must be, the meaning of this passage. An eternal and unconditional election is not, in the most distant form, referred to.

Matthew xxiv. 40, 41: "The one shall be taken and the other left." This passage simply asserts that, at the destruction of Jerusalem, one, in consequence of disregarding Christ's admonitions, would fall into the hands of the enemy, and the other, in consequence of heeding these admonitions, and "fleeing to the mountains," as directed, would escape. No referenced whatever to final salvation is had in the passage.

The only additional passage which requires notice is 2 Thess. ii. 13: "But we are bound to give thanks always to God for you, brethren, beloved of the Lord, because God hath from the beginning chosen you to salvation through sanctification of the Spirit and belief of the truth." One of the meanings very commonly attached to the original word here rendered "through," is "on account of, in consequence of." I will give a few examples. 1 Cor. xi. 17: "Now *in* this (on account of this) that I declare unto you, I praise you not." Acts vii. 29: "Then fled Moses *at* (on account of) this saying,"—the original term, here rendered "at," being the same as the one rendered *through*, in the passage under consideration. Mark ix. 41: "For whosoever shall give you a cup of water to drink *in* (on account of) my name, because ye belong to Christ." I might cite many more passages to the same purpose; but these are abundantly sufficient. That the term rendered *through*, in this passage, should be understood, in the sense of "on account of," or, "in consequence of," is perfectly manifest from the context. The apostle, in the preceding part of the chapter, is speaking of the fearful judgments which are to come upon incorrigible sinners, on account of their rejection of the truth. He then turns to the Christians of Thessalonica, to commend them for their faith. They, instead of imitating the example of wicked men, had obeyed the truth, through the Spirit; that is, had received, instead of rejection as incorrigible sinners do, the truth presented by the Spirit to their election. Hence he says: "But," that is, we have something of a far different nature to say of you, "we are bound to give thanks always to God for you, brethren, beloved of the Lord, because God hath from the beginning chosen you unto salvation, through (on account of) the sanctification of the Spirit, and belief of the truth;" that is, because you have been sanctified by the Spirit, by receiving by faith the truth which he has commended to your reception. For God, from the beginning, to determine to save all such as thus believe the truth, presented to their minds by his own Spirit, is quite another doctrine from that of an eternal unconditional election of a portion of sinners to life, while all might have been elected just as well, had God judged it wise so to do. The simple and exclusive object of the apostle, in this passage, is this: 1. To commend believers for their faith, and to impress them with a conviction of its infinite value, and preciousness in the sight of God. 2. As a means to this end, to remind them of God's gracious purpose in respect to them,—his purpose not to destroy them with the wicked, but to bestow upon them life eternal. Nothing is or can be, more foreign from his purpose, than the idea of thanking God that a portion of the race has been eternally and unconditionally elected to life, while the remainder are passed by, and left to perish in their sins. A more perverted construction cannot possibly be put upon a passage, than is put upon this, by turning it from its true original design, and making it teach such a soul-chilling doctrine. With two brief reflections I conclude this discourse.

1. We have, in the progress of our remarks, a very striking illustration of the tendency of a false theory, when once assumed as true, in blinding the mind to the real meaning of the Scriptures, and in preventing its even discerning their ineffable beauties, as well as in neutralizing the sanctifying power of their divine teachings upon the heart. All the passages which we have been considering, how long has their divine signification been thrown into a deep and dark eclipse, in consequence of their assumed relation to the doctrine of eternal and unconditional election and reprobation! How have their intrinsic beauties been veiled, and their otherwise sanctifying power become neutralized, by this means! Never will that "dearest of books"—the precious Bible—be to the world of mind what the sun is to the physical universe, unto its divine teachings are emancipated from the perversions of false systems of theology.

2. The aspect of the portion of Scripture which have been supposed to teach the doctrine of eternal and unconditional

election and reprobation, when seen in their true relations to the mind and the design of the Spirit in recording them, as contrasted with their appearance in their assumed relations to the doctrine under consideration, next claims our attention. When contemplated in their true light, they have a divine and ineffable beauty, and a most benign and sanctifying power. They breathe nothing but love, infinite as the love of God. They seem, and truly seem, to come warm from his infinite heart. The high Calvinist construction, on the other hand, throws them into the regions of eternal frost, and leaves in them one tendency and only one, a tendency to chill the soul and freeze up the fountain of life and love within it. What real virtue, actual or conceivable, has the dogma of eternal and unconditional election and reprobation,—the doctrine which makes the immortal destiny of moral beings turn wholly, not upon their own voluntary choice of life or death, but upon an eternal all-necessitating decree,—what real virtue has such a doctrine a tendency to develop in the human heart? Upon the sinner it can have no tendency but to palsy his powers into a fatal inaction, when he ought to be running for his life from the gates of death, or to cover his mind with the impenetrable gloom of despair. Upon the Christian it tends only to chill his sensibilities, pervert his ideas of a true moral government, and darken his apprehensions of God's judgments, as "true and righteous altogether." In the minds of all, alike, it tends only to render God an object of mere trembling awe and terror, instead of filial fear and reverence, adoptive trust, and confidence, and holy love.

LECTURE VI.

THE SPIRIT'S INFLUENCES.

ZECH. iv. 6.

"Not by might, nor by power, but by my Spirit, saith the God of Hosts."

EVERY system of religion, truly evangelical, ascribes the conversion of sinners to the Spirit of God, and maintains, throughout, the doctrine of salvation by grace. A difference of opinion obtains, only in respect to the *mode* of the Spirit's operations, and the relations of creatures of such operations. In the present discourse I propose to examine the various theories held by evangelical Christians on this subject,—theories, all of which, as far as my knowledge extends, may be included in the following enumeration:—

I. The first that I notice maintains the following propositions in respect to mankind as sinners:—

1. All mankind commence their moral agency, in consequence of the fall of our first parents, in a state of total inability to do anything good, or to avoid the acts of sin which they do, in fact perpetrate.

2. In the redemption of Christ provisions are made for a part of the race only, those whom God, from eternity, unconditionally elected to eternal life.

3. The influences of the Holy Spirit are exclusively confined to the elect, and his influence in respect to them are, in all cases, absolutely irresistible.

II. The second theory affirms the doctrine of total inability, and of the exclusive influence of the Spirit granted to the elect only; but asserts a general atonement for the sins of the race.

III. The third denies whole the doctrine of inability, affirms the universality of the atonement, but confines the influence of the Spirit exclusively to the elect.

IV. The fourth agrees, in all respects, with the last named, with this exception: it affirms that what are called the common influences of the Spirit—those from which conversion never does and never will result—are given to all; while his converting influences—those which, if imparted to all, would infallibly secure their conversion—are confined exclusively to the elect.

V. The fifth agrees with the two last named, in respect to the doctrines of ability and universal atonement, but denies that the Spirit now operates at all upon the human mind, either directly or through the truth. It confines the Spirit to the work of giving man revelation, and then leaves him, in the exercise of his own free agency, to determine his own destiny, by a voluntary acceptance or rejection of the truth thus revealed.

VI. The sixth and last theory that we are to consider, affirms the doctrines of man's freedom to good as well as evil, and of a universal atonement, denies the distinction between the common and converting influences of the Spirit, affirms that the Spirit is as universal in his influence as the atonement is in its provisions, and maintains that mankind are saved or lost only as they yield to or reject the truths presented to their minds through the word and Spirit of God. I shall consider these different theories in the order in which they are here presented.

I. In discussing the theory first named, I shall say nothing about the question whether the influences of the Spirit are confined exclusively to the elect, but shall reserve what I have to say upon this point till we advance to a consideration of the one next in order. As preparatory to a consideration of the elements of this theory, the following preliminary observations are deemed worthy of very special attention:—

1. This inability of the sinner to all that is good, attaches to him by no fault of his; inasmuch as it exists wholly independent of his personal agency. He had no more agency in its production than he had in the creation of the world. Grant, if you please, that it exists as the result of the Fall.

With that event, we, whose existence commenced some six thousand years subsequent to its occurrence, had no more to do with than with the murder of Abel. Any results following to us from either of these events, and following wholly independent of our knowledge, choice, or agency, we certainly, whoever else may be, are not responsible for. If, then, we are by nature wholly disabled to all good on the one hand, and to the avoidance of sin on the other, we are thus disabled by no fault of ours.

2. This inability exists, if it exists at all, as the result of the all-necessitating decree and agency of God. What is it that established the law of descent, so that, of necessity, the nature of the child is as that of the parent? The decree and agency of God. Whatever results from the necessary action of that law, results as the necessitated effect of the decree and agency of God. In 1 Cor. xv. 37, 38, we are informed that his is true of all the results of the law of generation in the vegetable creation. As God established and upholds this law, so he claims to be the author of all the results of the action of this law. "And that which thou sowest, thou sowest not that body that shall be, but bare grain, it may chance of wheat or of some other *grain*. But God giveth it a body as it hath please him, and to every seed his own body." If this be true of the law of vegetable production, it must be true of the law of generation among God's rational offspring. If the connection between the parent and the child is such, that the nature of the latter must be as that of the former, God established and upholds, by his own omnipotence, this connection, and is the author of the nature of the child, whatever it may be, whether it be sinful or holy, in the same sense, and for the same identical reason, that "He give to every seed its own body," in the vegetable world. No reasoning or sophistry can avoid this conclusion. If, then, we commence our being with a sinful nature, which absolutely disables us to all good, and renders it impossible for us to avoid sinning, God is the author of this nature, for the same reason, and in the same sense, that he is of the nature of plants. If Adam had a sinful nature, as the

pure result of his own act, it is God that so connects us with him that a sinful nature in us cannot but result from it. God, who established and now upholds this connection, is the sole author of all the results of that connection. Adam sinned, to be sure; but he had nothing to do with establishing and upholding the connection between him and his offspring. This, with all its results, God established, and he alone. Of the connection itself, then, and its results, he alone is the author. If a sinful nature in us is one of these results, God, and God alone, is the author of that nature.

3. It follows, as a necessary result of the proposition above established, that no one of the sons of Adam can perish, without being condemned to the endurance of eternal suffering for doing what, and for nothing else but what, God, by his own decree and agency, rendered it impossible for him not to do. The whole procedure of the divine administration rests upon this one principle, that of making creatures responsible for the unavoidable results of God's own decree and agency. Saints are taken to heaven, and sinners doomed to eternal death, for no other reason than this, being and doing what, and only what, God himself rendered it impossible for them not to be and do. We may safely challenge the world to show that these conclusions do not, from the laws of irreversible necessity, result from the fundamental elements of the theory now under consideration. I might safely leave the subject right here; for who can believe that God's eternal government rests upon such principles as these? I now advance, however, to a consideration of some additional objections which lie against two essential elements of this theory—the doctrine of inability, and of a limited atonement.

1. According to this theory, God has made a formal proposition to all the non-elect, that if they will perform an impossibility, he will perpetuate an act of injustice. That God has, in the most formal and positive manner, pledged himself to all sinners, the non-elect among the rest, that if they will repent he will forgive them their sins, no one will deny. "Let

the wicked" (that is, any wicked man on earth) "forsake his way, and the unrighteous man" (any unrighteous man, whether he be elect or non-elect) "his thoughts, and let him return unto the Lord, and he will have mercy upon him, and to our God, for he will abundantly pardon." . . . "Come now, and let us reason together, saith the Lord: though your sins be as scarlet, they shall be as white as snow; though they be red like crimson, they shall be as wool." This was said to individuals who, in fact, never did repent; that is, to some of the non-elect. Now, while God thus promises to all sinners that he will forgive them if they will repent, we are positively taught, Rom. iii. 26, that it would be unjust in God to forgive sin without an atonement. As, therefore, the sins of the non-elect, according to this theory, have never been atoned for, it would be unjust in God to forgive them, even if they did repent. What, then, is the proposition which God, in the most solemn and formal manner, has made to sinners, as far as the non-elect are concerned? It is this: If you will repent, that is, perform what is to you an absolute impossibility, I, on my part, though no atonement is made for you, will forgive you most graciously, and abundantly pardon you; that is, perpetrate an act of injustice. Such is the attitude in which this theory places God before the universe. Can such a theory be true? What higher evidence can we have that God has made provisions for the pardon of all men, than the fact that he has positively promised to forgive all men, if they will repent!

2. The entire procedure of the divine administration, according to this theory, rests upon a principle which, from the fixed and changeless laws of our mental constitution—laws which God has himself established—we cannot but affirm to be wrong. Suppose a thing has become to me, and that from no fault of mine, an impossibility. Is it possible for us to conceive, with the minds that God has given us, that I can be under obligation to perform, and justly condemned to the endurance of eternal vengeance for not performing, that impossible thing? According to the theory under

consideration, all the non-elect, by no fault of theirs, upon whomsoever the responsibility may rest, are possessed of a nature, and are placed in circumstances, which render it to them an absolute impossibility to do right, on the one hand, or not to do wrong, on the other. How can we conceive that they, on this supposition, can be under obligation to avoid the one and perform the other, and that they can be justly doomed to eternal agony for the non-performance of these impossibilities? God must reverse all the laws of our mental being, before he can bring his intelligent offspring to acquiesce in such principles of administration.

3. According to this theory, the entire moral government of God rests upon principles which all the world unite in denouncing as not only in themselves wrong, but the perfection of tyranny and injustice, when adopted by any other being but God. Nero, for example, issued edicts, but posted them where his subjects could not possibly read them, and then inflicted the severest penalties upon them for not obeying them. What has been the verdict of the universe upon him for the adoption of such principles of administration? And upon what grounds has that verdict rested? Upon this one exclusively,—that it is and must be wrong to require creatures to perform what is, and has to them, without any fault of theirs, become an impossibility. When men pronounce such judgments, they all unite in condemning the *principle* under consideration as in *itself* wrong. Does the entire moral government of God rest upon such a principle, and no other? It does, according to this theory. What must we think of the theory itself?

4. According to this theory, the non-elect are to be subject to sufferings infinitely aggravated, for rejecting offered mercy, when it was absolutely impossible for them, and God himself, as we have seen, had rendered it so,—when it was absolutely impossible for them, I say, to accept the offer, and when they could not have been saved had they done so. That the doom of sinners is to be infinitely aggravated, on account of their having rejected the offer of mercy through Christ, lies upon

the very surface of the Bible, and is a fact universally admitted. But this offer the non-elect have, according to this theory, no power to comply with; and, as no provisions for pardon exist, so far as they are concerned, they could not be forgiven if they should accept the offer. And yet their doom is to be eternally aggravated for "rejecting this great salvation." What do you think, hearer, of such a theory as that? Does it accord with what we cannot but know must be true of "the glorious gospel of the blessed God?"

5. The principles of this theory are opposed to the plainest and most obvious teaching of inspiration in respect to the extent of the atonement of Christ. What is the meaning of such declarations as these, pertaining to the design of the death and atonement of Christ? "And as Moses lifted up the serpent in the wilderness, even so must the Son of Man be lifted up; that whosoever believeth on him should not perish, but have eternal life. For God so loved the world, that he gave his only begotten Son, that whosoever believeth in him should not perish, but have everlasting life. For God sent not his Son into the world to condemn the world, but that the world through him might be saved." Nothing is said here about the elect in distinction from others. It is the *world* for whom Christ is here represented as making an atonement, and as coming to save. The object of his atonement is not that certain individuals of the race might be saved; but that "WHOSOEVER believeth in him might not perish, but have everlasting life." Such, again, 1 John ii. 2: "And he is the propitiation for our sins: and not for ours only, but also for *the sins of* the whole world." The term "our" here undeniably refers to believers. What, then, is meant by the words "the whole world?" Let us now read the first six verses of 1 Tim. ii.:—

"I exhort, therefore, that, first of all, supplications, prayers, intercessions, *and* giving of thanks be made for all men: for kings, and *for* all that are in authority; that we may lead a quiet and peaceable life in all godliness and honesty. For this is good and acceptable in the sight of God our Saviour, who will have all men to be saved, and to come unto the knowledge of the truth. For *there is* one God, and one mediator between God and men, the man Christ Jesus, who gave himself a ransom for all, to be testified in due time." In this whole passage the apostle makes no reference to the elect whatever. He is speaking of mankind indiscriminately. What, then, is his meaning, when he says that "Christ gave himself a ransom for *all?"* No unprejudiced mind can mistake the meaning of the term "all" in this connection. It must refer to every individual of the race. I forbear further citations, only adding, that if the Bible does not teach the doctrine of an unlimited atonement, it is one of the most unmeaning books that ever was written; and no doctrine whatever can be safely rested upon its teachings.

6. Equally opposed is the doctrine of the sinner's inability to do what is good, to the positive teachings of the Bible. The opposite doctrine is involved in the very words of the divine law itself. I will cite but a single passage in proof of this proposition, Luke x. 25—28: "And, behold, a certain lawyer stood up, and tempted him, saying, Master, what shall I do to inherit eternal life? He said unto him, What is written in the law! how readest thou? And he answering said, Thou shalt love the Lord thy God with all thy heart, and with all thy soul, and with all thy strength, and with all thy mind; and thy neighbor as thyself. And he said unto him, Thou hast answered right: this do, and thou shalt live." All that God requires of creatures, as we are told elsewhere, is "comprehended in one word—love." "Love is the fulfilling of the law." In the passage above cited, we are most positively taught that the *extent* of the demands of this law is limited by the power or ability of the creature. "With *all thy strength;"* that is, with all the ability you actually possess, and with no more, and no lees. A theory, that thus stands opposed to all the affirmations of reason and revelation alike, pertaining to the subject, we certainly run no risk in departing from the truth when we reject.

II. We will now consider the second theory named above,—the theory which agrees with the one which we have just considered, excepting in one particular, the extent of the atonement. It affirms a universal atonement for the race, but denies its universal availableness to all men, and that for two reasons,—the sinner's absolute inability, in himself, to accept of the provisions of grace, in the first instance, and because the Spirit is totally withheld from the non-elect, in the next. On this theory I remark,

1. It is in itself most palpably self-contradictory. Provisions of which we cannot possibly avail ourselves are, in fact, no provisions at all; and it is a contradiction in terms to call them so. They are nothing but a solemn mockery of our misery. Suppose, to take a borrowed illustration, that government requires a man to run a train of cars from London to Liverpool; it lays down a most perfect track, provides the train and the engine, and furnishes the requisite fuel and water, but withholds the fire requisite to light the fuel and heat the water, that the train may be put in motion, and that while it is absolutely impossible for the subject to get the fire elsewhere, or to run the train without it. Has government made provisions for running the train from London to Liverpool? So, if God has provided the means of pardon, but withheld his Spirit, without whose aid it is impossible for us to avail ourselves of such provisions, they are in fact no provisions for us, and it is a contradiction in terms to call them such.

2. The provisions of grace and offers of mercy are, according to this theory, no acts of kindness to the non-elect, but an infinite calamity to them, and that from no fault of theirs. Is it kind to offer a remedy to an individual, when it is impossible for him not to reject it, and when his misery must be eternally aggravated by the offer itself? According to this theory, God, in the first instance, by establishing and upholding the laws of natural generation, imparts to the non-elect a nature which renders it impossible for them not to sin. In the next place, he

makes an atonement for their sins. He then presents the offer of life to them, under circumstances which render it absolutely impossible for them not to reject the offer. He then, to all eternity, renders their doom infinitely aggravated, because they have done that which by no possibility they could avoid, to wit, rejected offered mercy. Where is the love or kindness in presenting such an offer to creatures placed, without their own election, in such circumstances? What an infinite calamity, instead of kindness, is the death of Christ to all such! Is this "the glorious gospel of the blessed God?"

3. This theory contradicts the positive teachings of the Scriptures in respect to the extent of the Spirit's influences. If the Holy Spirit is never, as this theory asserts, given to any but the elect, then none of our race ever did, or ever can, "resist the Holy Ghost." The non-elect cannot do it, because he never strives with them; the elect cannot do it, because he operates upon them irresistibly. Such are the teachings of this theory on this subject. Now, Christians are required and exhorted not to grieve and quench the Holy Spirit. This implies that his influence, even in their case, may be resisted. Sinners, also, who never repented, were charged with "resisting the Holy Ghost." "Ye do ALWAYS resist the Holy Ghost. As your fathers did so do ye." How strange that, in the presence of such declarations, a theory of divine influence should be farmed which confines the Spirit's influence to those who are truly converted! When will Christians let the Bible teach them theology, instead of first framing a system of theology, and then warping and perverting the word of God, to make it accord with such a system? What pupil of the Holy Spirit would ever gather, from what he meets with on the sacred page, that God's Spirit is partial in his influence? But does not "the wind blow where it listeth," and is it not said that "so is every one that is born of the Spirit?" Truly the wind thus bloweth. But is it partial in its influence? Does it not, when it blows, strike all alike? "So is every one that is born of the Spirit." The last idea that such a representation is adapted to convey is this, that the believer is converted by an influence

given to him and withheld from others. Precisely the opposite truth is conveyed by these words. The object of the Saviour was to teach Nicodemus that the sinner is converted by an invisible internal influence operating upon the heart, in opposition to the Jewish notion of a birth to life eternal by natural generation, or some outward arrangement depending upon the will of man. But nothing is further from his design than to teach that this influence is partial, or limited in its operations. The illustration used is adapted only to the expression of the opposite idea.

III. The theory which next claims our attention differs from the one last named only in respect to the doctrine of inability. It asserts the ability or free agency of man, maintains the doctrine of universal atonement, but limits the influences of the Spirit to the elect. The following are all the considerations deemed requisite to urge against such a theory as this,—considerations bearing exclusively upon the one single point, the principle that the Spirit's influences are limited to the elect.

1. This theory has no authority whatever in a single passage of the Bible. Where, within the lids of the word of God, is there a single passage that asserts, or intimates, or says anything that implies, that the influences of the Spirit are given to a part of the race, and withheld from the rest? No one, I am confident, will presume to attempt to prove such a dogma from any of the positive teachings of inspiration on the subject. How little fundamental reference is there to the Bible in the formation of systems of theology!

2. It is as unreasonable in itself, and as contrary to our ideas of the infinite, universal, and impartial love of God, to suppose that the atonement is limited, as it is to suppose that God's Spirit is partial in his influences. From what element of the divine character, from what principle of his eternal government, or from what aspect of the great atonement, can such an idea be discovered?

3. The idea of a universal atonement, through the second person of the Trinity, is wholly repugnant in itself to that of a

limited divine influence, to accomplish the ends of that atonement, through the third person. Why should the love of God to the world be less universal and impartial, as manifested through the mission of the third, than through that of the second person of the Trinity? Nothing but the exigency of a false theory can place the mission of the Spirit in such unnatural and repulsive relations to that of the Son of God.

4. The same mode of reasoning by which we could derive from the Scriptures the doctrine of partialism, as far as the Spirit is concerned, would be equally conclusive against a general atonement. This statement is self-evident, and needs no further elucidation.

5. This theory, as we have already seen, is contradicted by the positive teachings of the Holy Scriptures. If the Bible teaches anything, it teaches the great truth that sinners perish, not because they never had the Spirit, but because "they do always resist the Holy Ghost."

6. But I have yet another objection, if possible of still greater weight, against this theory. That God sincerely desires that all men should accept the offer of mercy through Christ, the Bible most abundantly teaches, and all the advocates of this theory admit; if he withholds his Spirit from all who are not finally saved, then his sincere desire is that they, without the Spirit, should accept of mercy and be saved. God, then, sincerely desires that a part of mankind should enter heaven, through the united agency of all the persons in the Trinity, and a part share this same blessedness through the agency of but two of them. Where is the reason for such a desire as that, and what must we think of a theory that places the infinite God in such a relation as that to his creatures?

IV. The fourth theory that we are to consider, agrees in all respects with the one last named, with this exception: it affirms that what are called the *common* influences of the Spirit,—those from which conversion never does and never will result, are given to all; while his *converting* influences, —those which, if imparted to all, would infallibly secure their conversion, are confined exclusively to the elect. Now, against this theory I urge the following, to me, unanswerable objections:—

1. The distinction under consideration has no authority from the Bible. Where does the Bible speak of the common *non-converting*, and of the special *converting*, influences of the Spirit? Where does it intimate that those influences which the incorrigible sinner resists to his own destruction, are not the same as those to which the believer yields when he is converted? We shall search in vain, among all the teachings of God's Spirit in his word, for the distinction under consideration.

2. This distinction is made in opposition to the most plain and positive teachings of the Bible. I will adduce a single passage in proof of this proposition. I refer to Isaiah v. 1—5: "Now will I sing to my well-beloved a song of my beloved," &c.

Three important facts pertaining to this affecting parable demand our special attention. (1.) The representation is, that all that is ever done for vineyards which actually bring forth good fruit, had been done for this yard. (2.) Under the very circumstances and influences under which one vineyard bears good fruit, this brought forth wild grapes. (3.) Under these identical circumstances and influences, the prospect of its bearing good fruit became hopeless.

This parable is used for the avowed purpose of illustrating and exemplifying God's dealings with sinners who continue incorrigible under all his efforts for their salvation, and finally perish in their sins. In the presence of the perishing sinner, God put the question, What could I have done, to prevent his death, that I have not done? Where would there be any propriety to such a question, if a divine and all-converting influence, granted to others, had been withheld from him, and he had been subject to those influences only from which conversion never does and never will result?

3. All the representations of the Bible, pertaining to the reasons for the salvation of believers on the one hand, and for the destruction of the finally incorrigible on the other, are wholly incompatible with the distinction under consideration. The sinner is represented as perishing for rejecting the identical Saviour which the Christian is saved for believing in, and for resisting the same Spirit to whose divine influence the believer yields in conversion. The Saviour and the Spirit both have their mission in the world. The destiny of men turns upon their voluntary reception or rejection of each alike in the fulfilment of his mission.

4. The common influences of the Spirit given to men, while the special converting ones are withheld, are nothing but an infinite calamity to the sinner, and can have been given but to aggravate his doom. They answer no other purpose, and cannot be given for the purpose of securing the salvation of him who is subject to them. For what purpose, then, can they be given, but to answer the end they do answer, to aggravate the doom of the sinner?

5. All that the Bible says of the divine forbearance is in opposition to this theory. This forbearance is affirmed to be exercised for one special purpose, the actual conversion and salvation of men. Does God continue men subject to influences under which no man ever did or ever will repent, and that for the sincere purpose of securing their repentance under those influences? I cannot believe that such is the character of God's dispensations towards his rational offspring. God never acts for the avowed purpose of realizing a given end, and acts in the exclusive use of means which, in no solitary instance, result in securing that end.

V. We now come to a consideration of the theory next in order, that which agrees with the one last mentioned in respect to the doctrines of ability and universal atonement, but denies that the Spirit *now* operates at all upon the human mind, either directly or through the truth; the theory which confines the office of the Spirit to the work of *giving a revelation* to man, and affirms that he is then left, in the exercise of his own free agency, to determine his own destiny, by a voluntary reception or rejection of the truth thus revealed. In regard to this theory I remark—

1. It confines the Spirit's influences to inspired teachers; whereas the Scriptures represent him as given to the *entire Church*. All alike are commanded to be filled with the Spirit. Eph. v. 18.

2. This theory contradicts the express language of our Saviour, when he gave the promise of the Spirit. The Spirit was not to come into the world and perform a certain work, and then leave the world, as Christ himself was to do, but was to abide with his people *forever*. John xiv. 16.

3. The Spirit is represented as given to believers *after* they have understood and received the "word of truth," and given as the seal or divine token of their adoption, and as an earnest or foretaste of their future inheritance. Eph. i. 13, 14: "In whom ye also trusted," &c.

4. God is represented as dwelling in, and as communing with, his people through the Spirit,—a truth wholly inconsistent with the theory under consideration. Eph. ii. 13, 22: "But now in Christ Jesus ye who sometimes were afar off," &c.

5. The Spirit is represented as *aiding* Christians in prayer; a *present* work, and one very different from that of merely giving a revelation, and then leaving the people of God, and the world too, to find out the truth, and address a throne of grace as they may. Rom. viii. 26. I need add no further considerations on this point. A theory which stands in such direct and palpable opposition to the express teachings of inspiration on the subject, cannot surely accord with the mind of the Spirit.

VI. The sixth and last theory to be considered, next claims our attention. According to this theory, the mission of the Spirit is wholly subsidiary to that of Christ, and is coëxtensive with it in design and actual influence. As "Christ tasted death for EVERY man," so the mission of the

Spirit is to bring every man under an influence best adapted to secure to him an acceptance of the provisions of mercy. As no sinner perishes without an atonement, so none perish only as they have resisted the Spirit of God pressing the provisions of grace upon their acceptance. As no provisions are made for a part and withheld from the rest, so there are no common unconverting influences of the Spirit given to a part, and serving in their case, consequent on their intrinsic inefficiency, no other purpose but to fit men for perdition; and special converting influences, which, if given to all, would infallibly secure their conversion, but which God, in his sovereignty, withholds from the many and bestows upon the few. It is not affirmed that the Spirit does not operate at one time more than another, or equally upon all. But it is maintained that all his influences, as far as sinners are concerned, are, in fact, converting influences,—influeuces under which conversion not only may, but, in many instances, actually does take place. Sinners are not to be exhorted to pray for the Spirit to convert them, but to yield to his influences at once, in the exercise of "repentance toward God, and faith toward our Lord Jesus Christ." The office of the Spirit is to present the truth to the mind of the sinner. The work, and the only work, of the sinner is, not to pray for the Spirit, but to yield at once to the truth presented by the Spirit to his mind. The office of the religious teacher is, not first to tell the sinner of his dependence upon the Spirit, and then to exhort him to pray for the converting influences of the Spirit, but to urge him at once to yield to the Spirit by embracing the truth. In fulfilling his mission, the Spirit, according to this theory, sustains two relations entirely distinct to mankind,—one to sinners, and the other to believers. In his relations to the former, his office is to "convince THE WORLD of sin, of righteousness, and of judgment." In his relations to the latter, he opens upon the mental vision the things of Christ, that "we all, (with open face,) beholding as in a glass the glory of the Lord, may be changed into the same image from glory to glory, even as by the Spirit of the Lord." To the sinner he comes unasked. To the believer he is given in answer to prayer. The "sealing and earnest of the Spirit" are to be sought by faith, just as pardon through Christ is thus sought. "How much more shall our Father who is in heaven give the Holy Spirit to them that ask him!" A few considerations only are requisite to show that this is the true view of this great subject.

1. In showing that all the other theories are and must be false, the highest evidence has been presented of the truth of that now under consideration.

2. The mission of the Spirit, in each of the forms above named, is a clearly revealed fact. The distinction between his common unconverting, and his special converting, influences, as a fact, is nowhere revealed, or even directly or indirectly hinted at, in the Bible. When we make such a distinction, "we are wise above what is written."

3. The absolute universality and impartiality of the *provisions* of grace, through Christ, demand the supposition that the Spirit, in his mission, based wholly as it is upon such provisions, will be equally universal and impartial. As there are no provisions of grace for a part of the race fully adequate for their necessities, and other provisions for the rest inadequate for theirs so it is infinitely unreasonable to suppose that there are common unconverting influences of the Spirit given to a part, and special converting influences given to the rest, and in God's sovereignty withheld from all the world besides. What can be more unreasonable, without an express revelation to the contrary, than the supposition that the love of God to the race, manifested through the mission of the Spirit, is less universal and impartial than that manifested through the mission of Christ! Such an idea supposes a total want of harmony, among the persons of the Trinity, in the work of redemption. The Father is represented as "willing that all men should be saved," and, from "love to the WORLD," as giving the Son to "taste death for every man." In the name of every person of the Trinity, he takes an oath that "he is not willing

that any should perish." Christ, in conformity to the plans and principles of such a form of love,—love absolutely universal and impartial,—makes provisions coextensive with the wants of universal humanity. The Spirit now appears as the final expression and manifestation of this love; and what, according to this idea, does he do? He gives converting influences to a part of the race,—influences which, if given to all, would infallibly secure their conversion,—and by an act of sovereignty withholds such influences from the rest. Where is the divine harmony in the relations of the different persons of the Trinity to the work of redemption, on such a supposition?

4. Nothing but the exigencies of a pre-formed theory pertaining to conversion, and not a simple study of what the Spirit has himself revealed in regard to his own mission, ever led (am I not justified in affirming?) to the distinction between the unconverting and converting influences of the Spirit. Now, whenever our theories lead us to discriminate where the Bible does not make a difference, it is quite safe and becoming in us to question the truth of our speculations.

5. The theory under consideration accords with the positive teachings of the Bible. I need only refer, is confirmation of this proposition, to what was said under a former head, on the parable of the vineyard, found in Isaiah v. 1—5. Suppose that God, by an Act of sovereignty, withholds from all who are finally lost a divine influence, which, if given, would infallibly secure their conversion, and then, in the presence of such a fact, asks the question, What could I do, to prevent the doom of these men, that I am not doing? The answer is ready. Such a question can never properly be put, on any other supposition than the truth of the theory of divine influence before us. Wherever, also, we read that some are saved, in consequence of "obeying the truth through the Spirit," and others lost, consequent on "resisting the Holy Ghost," we are bound to suppose, without an express revelation to the contrary, that the influence yielded to on the one hand, and resisted on the other, is one and the same.

6. This theory, and this alone, perfectly meets our ideas of what *ought* to be under the divine government. If creatures are saved and lost in the presence of the same provisions, and under influences precisely similar, and are saved or lost, only as they voluntarily accept and yield to, or resist and reject, such provisions and influences, then every department of our moral nature is satisfied with the divine dispensations. Every department of our better nature, on the other hand, naturally and necessarily revolts from every other view.

7. Finally, this theory, and this alone, accords fully with the *manner* in which men, under the influence of the Spirit, present the truth to sinners. Such men never, in any solitary instance, tell the sinner of his dependence upon the sovereign agency of the Spirit for conversion, and then exhort him to pray for the converting influences of the Spirit. How individuals dare to adopt such a mode of teaching, and that in direct opposition to inspired example, is a perfect mystery to me. On the other hand, inspired men always address sinners directly on the duty of immediate "*repentance* toward God, and *faith* toward our Lord Jesus Christ;" and they are then exhorted to yield at once to the Spirit by obeying the truth, and charged with "resisting the Holy Ghost" while they refuse to do it. No other form of teaching has the least shadow of sanction from inspired example. Instead of exhorting the sinner, remaining impenitent, to pray for the Spirit to convert him, he is expressly informed that unless he "prays in nothing wavering," he is not to "expect to receive anything from God." Now, the theory under consideration perfectly accords with such a mode of teaching, and it is the only theory that does accord with it. What higher evidence can be demanded of its truth?

REMARKS.

1. It is no objection to the theory of divine influence, established in this lecture, that the Bible ascribes the difference between believers and unbelievers to the Spirit and

grace of Christ. The Christian is what he is "by the grace of God," and "has nothing but what he has received." If the question be asked, however, *why* has he, and *why* has the sinner not, this grace? the Bible answer to the question is this: The one has this grace because he voluntarily received it by faith, or "obeyed the truth through the Spirit," and the other has it not, because he "put" the same grace "from him."

2. We have, in the manner in which the doctrine of the Spirit's influences are very commonly presented, a striking exemplification of the fact that, under the influence of a certain theory relative to any given subject, men, professing a supreme reverence for the Scriptures, will frequently run directly over their most manifest teachings on that subject. I hold it to be a truth self-evident, and the opposite as a most dangerous error, that we are bound, not only to teach *what* is revealed in the "law and the testimony," but to conform our *manner* of teaching to clearly revealed inspired example. In traversing this kingdom, I find a quite common impression to exist, that a sermon is hardly evangelical in which the sinner is not reminded of his dependence upon the Spirit for conversion, and exhorted to pray for the Spirit to impart to him a converting influence. What is the intrinsic tendency of such a mode of teaching? To turn the attention of sinner away from the very duty which it is the exclusive object of inspiration to fix it upon, to wit, the duty of immediate repentance toward God, and faith toward our Lord Jesus Christ, and to prevent his yielding to the Spirit, by obeying his call to "repentance and faith." It tends, also, to impress the sinner with an error most unscriptural, and of most dangerous tendency, to wit, that prayer put up in impenitence and unbelief will be acceptable to God. Such a mode of presenting the doctrine of divine influence, also, is in express and open opposition to inspired example. Nothing like this, but everything in opposition to it, appears every where in the example of inspired teachers. Instead of telling the sinner of his dependence upon the Spirit, they tell him that he is "*always* resisting the Holy Ghost" while he remains

unconverted. Instead of telling him to pray for the Spirit, they urge him not to resist the Spirit by refusing to "obey the truth." If we would follow inspired example, both in respect to manner and matter, we shall not, by our teaching, lead sinners to inquire "who shall ascend into heaven," or "go over the sea," or "descend into the deep," to bring Christ or the Spirit to us. On the other hand, teaching them that "the word is very nigh them, even in their mouth and in their heart," we shall urge them at once to yield to the word and Spirit, by "laying," directly and immediately, "hold upon the hope set before them."

APPENDIX I.

LISTING OF WORKS BY ASA MAHAN.
Partly available online, in CD and print format from Alethea In Heart.
http://TruthInHeart.com

Books.

- The System of Mental Philosophy. 1882. 285 pages.

- The Science of Intellectual Philosophy. 1854. 476 pages.

- Critical History of Philosophy in Two Volumes. 1883. 1000 pages.

- The Science of Natural Theology: God the Infinite and Perfect seen in Creation. 1867. 399 pages.

- The Doctrine of the Will. 1847. 233 pages.

- Science of Moral Philosophy. 1848. 420 pages.

- The Science of Logic; or An Analysis of the Law of Thought. 1857. 400 pages.

- **Autobiography: Intellectual, Moral, and Spiritual.** Focuses on the effects of Calvinism; pastoral education, and higher life experience. 1882. 458 pages.

- **Out of Darkness Into Light.** 1878. Mahan's detailed description of his spiritual journey.

- **Baptism of the Holy Ghost.** A doctrinal overview. 1875. 180 pages.

- **Misunderstood Texts.** Expounding anti-holiness proof-texts at the recommendation of Moses Stuart. 1876. 110 pages.

- Christian Perfection. 1837, 1875. 156 pages.

- Lectures on the 9th of Romans. Election and the Influence of the Holy Spirit. 1859. 180 pages.

- The Phenomena of Spiritism: Scientifically Explained and Examined. Expositing Modern Mysteries of unusual phenomena, tricksters, etc. 1875. 421 pages.

- Modern Mysteries Explained and Exposed: In four parts. As above volume; divine authority of the bible. 1855. 466 pages.

- A Critical History of the Late American War. 1877. (See how Mahan almost prevented half a million deaths!) 461 pages.

- The True Believer. From *The Oberlin Evangelist*. 1847. 240 pages.

- Life Thoughts on the Rest of Faith. 1872. 224 pages.

Articles.

- Theism and Anti-Theism in the Relations to Science: From *The Ingham lectures.* 1873. 30 pages.

- Experience of President Mahan: In a letter to his wife.

- Gospel Plan: A sermon from *The Oberlin Evangelist* and *The True Believer.*

- The Believers Confidence: A Sermon from *The Oberlin Evangelist* and *The True Believer.*

- Dr. Mahan's Speech on the Crisis in the Protestant Episcopal Church in America. 1862.

- The Relation of Christianity in the Freedom of Human Thought and Action. Lecture for the YMCA. 1840. 43 pages.

- **Reform.** True Liberality—Intolerance of Reform. From *The Obelin Evangelist.*

- The Natural and the Supernatural in the Christian Life and Experience. 1878.

- Physical and Moral Law Obligatory. 1839. 8 pages.

Mahan's Articles from The Oberlin Quarterly Review.

- **The Book of Job.** Notes Critical (By Albert Barnes), Illustrative, and Practical, on the Book of Job, with a new Translation, and an Introductory Dissertation. 33 pages.

- **The Book of Ecclesiastes.** 26 pages.

- **Brotherly Love:** Deals with the complexities of fellowship and disfellowship.

- **Principles of Church Discipline.** 1848. 15 pages.

- **The Sufferings of Christ.** Did Christ suffer in his Infinite Nature or just in his human nature?

- **Solomon's Song.** A unique analysis and critique of standard interpretations.

- **The Idea of Retribution.** 1848. 13 pages.

- **The Tree of Knowledge of Good and Evil.** 1848. 8 p.

- **Doctrine of Resurrection.** 1848. 14 pages.

- The Confession of Faith of the Presbyterian Church. 1848. 26 p

- Moses. 1848. 30 pages.

- The Doctrine of Imperfection. 1848. 21 pages.

Periodicals and Miscellaneous Notes.

Mahan also wrote extensively in America and England in Periodicals: *The Oberlin Evangelist; The Oberlin Quarterly Review; Banner of Holiness;* and *Divine Life and International Expositor,* 1877-1889)— all of which he edited. There also is a 'Notebook' of Miscellaneous notes found at Adrian College in Michigan where he served his third presidency (which we have photographed). With the help of our friends we hope to republish these works and many other lectures found elsewhere.

If you would like to help with this project contact us at: rickfriedrich@hotmail.com

Published Biographical Information about Mahan.

- **Modern Oberlin College Biographical Account**.

- **Autobiography of Asa Mahan.** (see above)

- **Out of Darkness Into Light**. (see above)

- **Oberlin. Its origin, progress and results.** An address, prepared for the alumni of Oberlin college, assembled August 22, 1860. By James H. Fairchild (3rd President of Oberlin College). 88 pages.

- **The Memoirs of Charles Grandison Finney.** By Charles G. Finney. Professor in Oberlin Theological Seminary. 1891.

- **The Life of Charles G. Finney.** By A. M. Hills. 1902. Mahan's Resignation and Oberlin's Spiritual Decline: Rev. Sherlock Bristol's Letter to A. M. Hills. From Hills' Biography of Finney. Bristol was of the second graduating class at Oberlin, and shared with Mahan the experience of the Baptism of the Holy Spirit.

- **Charles Grandison Finney.** By George Frederick Wright, D. D., LL. D. Professor in Oberlin Theological Seminary. 1891.

- **Oberliniana.** A Jubilee Volume of Semi-Historical Anecdotes connected with the past and present of OBERLIN COLLEGE. 1833-1883. By A. L. Shumway, and C. DeW. Brown. 175 pages.

- **Mahan the first President of Cleveland University** .

Letters of Asa Mahan.

- **Ex-President Letters.** 1872. 32 pages.

- **Letter to Abraham Lincoln.**

Recent Writings About Mahan.
(Available on our website: Truthinheart.com)

- **Freedom and Grace**: The Life of Asa Mahan. By Edward H. Madden and James E. Hamilton. Metuchen, New Jersey: The Scarecrow Press, Inc., 1982. 273 pages.

- **Book Review of: Freedom and Grace**: The Life of Asa Mahan. By Edward H. Madden and James E. Hamilton. Metuchen, New Jersey: The Scarecrow Press, Inc., 1982. 273 pp. Reviewed by Harold E. Raser. "The latest offering in the important 'Studies in Evangelicalism' series under the guidance of Kenneth Rowe and Donald Dayton is this long needed biography of Asa Mahan. Edward Madden, now retired from teaching at the State University of New York (Buffalo), and his former graduate student, James Hamilton, now of the Asbury

College Philosophy Department, have collaborated to produce the first full-length critical study of a person who, though his life spanned nearly the whole of the nineteenth century and he played a central role in some of the most significant American religious, intellectual, and social movements of that century, has yet been strangely neglected in the chronicling of the prominent. His close associate and friend, Charles Finney, has captured the scholars' attention much more often. Mahan's many writings have been readily available, his Autobiography: Intellectual, Moral and Spiritual (1882) being a primary biographical source, but students of American history are only now beginning to mine the unpublished collections housed at Oberlin College and elsewhere, and to offer scholarly assessments of Mahan."

- **The Church as a Universal Reform Society :** The Social Vision of Asa Mahan. By James E. Hamilton.

- **Nineteenth Century Philosophy and Holiness Theology:** A Study in the Thought of Asa Mahan. By James E. Hamilton.

- **Epistemology and Theology in American Methodism.** By James E. Hamilton.

- **Asa Mahan and the Development of American Holiness Theology.** By Donald W. Dayton.

- **The Historiography of the Wesleyan/Holiness Tradition.** By David Bundy.

- **The Doctrine of the Sanctifying Spirit:** Charles G. Finney's Synthesis of Wesleyan and Covenant Theology. By Timothy L. Smith.

- **The Doctrine of the Baptism of the Holy Spirit:** Its Emergence and Significance. By Timothy L. Smith.

- **The Baptism of the Holy Spirit in the Wesleyan Tradition.** By George Allen Turner.

www.ingramcontent.com/pod-product-compliance
Lightning Source LLC
Chambersburg PA
CBHW071715090426
42738CB00009B/1781